Catching

Fire

Becoming

Flame

TENTH ANNIVERSARY EDITION

Swimming in the Sun: Rediscovering the Lord's Prayer with Francis of Assisi and Thomas Merton (St. Anthony Messenger Press, 1993)

Enkindled: Holy Spirit, Holy Gifts, coauthored with Bridget Haase, OSU (St. Anthony Messenger Press, 2001)

Instruments of Christ: Reflections on the Peace Prayer of St. Francis of Assisi (St. Anthony Messenger Press, 2004)

Coming Home to Your True Self: Leaving the Emptiness of False Attractions (InterVarsity Press, 2008)

Living the Lord's Prayer: The Way of the Disciple (InterVarsity Press, 2009)

The Lord's Prayer: A Summary of the Entire Gospel (Five CDs) (Learn25.com, 2010)

This Sacred Moment: Becoming Holy Right Where You Are (InterVarsity Press, 2011)

The Life of Antony of Egypt: by Athanasius, A Paraphrase (InterVarsity Press, 2012)

Catching Fire, Becoming Flame: A Guide for Spiritual Transformation (Paraclete Press, 2013)

Catching Fire, Becoming Flame: A Guide for Spiritual Transformation (DVD and Streaming Video) (Paraclete Press, 2013)

Keeping the Fire Alive: Navigating Challenges in the Spiritual Life (DVD and Streaming Video) (Paraclete Press, 2014)

Come, Follow Me: Six Responses to the Call of Jesus (DVD and Streaming Video) (Paraclete Press, 2014)

Saying Yes: Discovering and Responding to God's Will in Your Life (Paraclete Press, 2016)

Saying Yes: What is God's Will for Me? (DVD and Streaming Video) (Paraclete Press, 2016)

The BE Attitudes: Ten Paths to Holiness (DVD and Streaming Video) (Paraclete Press, 2019)

Practical Holiness: Pope Francis as Spiritual Companion (Paraclete Press, 2019)

Becoming an Ordinary Mystic: Spirituality for the Rest of Us (InterVarsity Press, 2019)

Soul Training with the Peace Prayer of Saint Francis (Franciscan Media, 2020)

Sundays on the Go: 90 Seconds with the Weekly Gospel, Year A (Paraclete Press, 2022)

ALBERT HAASE, OFM

Catching

Fire

Becoming

A GUIDE FOR SPIRITUAL
TRANSFORMATION

Flame

REVISED & EXPANDED
TENTH ANNIVERSARY EDITION

PARACLETE PRESS
Brewster, Massachusetts

2022 First Printing This Edition
Catching Fire, Becoming Flame: A Guide for Spiritual Transformation
Tenth Anniversary Edition

Copyright © 2023 by Franciscan Friars of the State of Missouri
ISBN 978-1-64060-861-0

Unless otherwise noted, Scripture references are taken the New Revised Standard Version Bible: Catholic Edition copyright © 1993 and 1989 by the Division of Christian Education of the National Council of the Churches of Christ in the United States of America, and are used by permission. All rights reserved.

Scripture references marked MSG are taken from *The Message.* Copyright © 1993, 1994, 1995, 1996, 2000, 2001, 2002. Used by permission of NavPress Publishing Group.

Two paragraphs of Chapter 6 were taken from Albert Haase, OFM, *Becoming an Ordinary Mystic: Spirituality for the Rest of Us* (Downers Grove IL: InterVarsity Press, 2019), 48–50 and one paragraph from Albert Haase, OFM, *Soul Training with the Peace Prayer of Saint Francis* (Cincinnati, OH: Franciscan Media, 2020), 38–39.

Library of Congress Cataloging-in-Publication Data is available

10 9 8 7 6 5 4 3 2 1

Published by Paraclete Press Brewster, Massachusetts
www.paracletepress.com
Printed in the United States of America

Abba Lot went to see Abba Joseph and said to him, "Abba, as far as I can, I say my little office, I fast a little, I pray and meditate, I live in peace and as far as I can, I purify my thoughts. What else can I do?" Then the old man stood up and stretched his hands toward heaven.

His fingers became like ten lamps of fire and he said to him, "If you will, you can become all flame."

—*The Sayings of the Desert Fathers*

CONTENTS

Fanning The Flame
DISCERNMENT

Becoming All Flame
DYNAMIC COMMITMENTS

STILL BURNING

∎

This tenth anniversary edition of *Catching Fire, Becoming Flame: A Guide for Spiritual Transformation* has given me cause to pause and ponder. Why has this book and the two DVDs (now streaming videos) associated with it, *Catching Fire, Becoming Flame: A Guide for Spiritual Transformation* and *Keeping the Fire Alive: Navigating Challenges in the Spiritual Life*, been so immensely popular? Never in my wildest dreams did I ever think they would become the bestsellers they have become.

I still remember the woman who gave me the idea for the book and videos. I was giving a workshop on the spiritual journey at a church in the suburbs of Chicago. During the lunch break, she approached. "Father," she said, "your presentations today are so enlightening and informative. For years I've been hankering for spirituality resources. Many churches offer Bible studies for their parishioners and that's wonderful. But some of us are interested in spiritual formation and spirituality studies. Just look at all these people who have shown up for your workshop today. Why don't you think about putting your knowledge and experience with the spiritual life into a book and maybe even film some videos that people interested in spirituality could watch together?"

This woman was fanning some embers deep within me. I too had often wondered why there were no spirituality resources available for people like myself who burned with an interest in the spiritual life. That very night, after returning to the friary, even though I was dead tired and mentally exhausted, I turned on my computer and started listing topics that I thought would be essential and helpful for someone interested in the spiritual life. It took me two weeks to decide on the material that should be included. I thought of this emerging book as a "literary" spiritual director that people could turn to as they explored their relationship with God. I also wanted it to be a compendium of what I had learned about the spiritual life after fanning God's spark since my teenage years.

Over the past decade, I've given workshops on the contents of this book across the United States, Canada, and Singapore. I've also received hundreds of emails thanking me for this book and its streaming videos. I've been told they have been used as an alternative to Bible studies in both Catholic and Protestant churches. They're currently being used in training programs for permanent deacons and spiritual directors. Seminaries are suggesting them for the formation of people preparing for ministry, and many religious orders are using them in the formation of their novices.

I was humbled and delighted when Paraclete Press approached me about the possibility of offering a tenth anniversary edition of this book. Over the years as I have returned to the original edition, I saw some gaps that needed to be filled. As a result, I have included five additional chapters to this anniversary edition that deal with the living flame of love, the Jesus Prayer, inner healing, hospitality, and living in the present moment. I also have tweaked the content of some chapters since my understanding of the spiritual life and spiritual formation has shifted and hopefully matured.

I made the decision to delete the "Go Deeper" section that concluded each chapter of the original edition. Some of the recommended resources have gone out of print while others are so old that it would be impossible to retrieve them. The chapters in this tenth anniversary edition reflect the latest insights and perennial wisdom found in those suggested resources.

Jesus said, "I came to bring fire to the earth, and how I wish it were already kindled!" (Luke 12:49) It is my hope that the tenth anniversary edition of this book will help you prepare kindling in your hearth that will catch fire with love for the things of heaven, the wonders of creation, and the people of earth. May we never tire of fanning that flame and keeping it burning.

Albert Haase, OFM
Feast of Pentecost

GOD'S PASSION, OUR ENTHUSIASM

■

My friend Helen is the mother of two daughters. She's a retired executive assistant for a senior partner in a global financial services firm. She's a good wife, an honest woman, and a faithful friend. She's also dedicated to her faith and committed to working on her relationship with God. I nodded in agreement when I heard someone say, "You can feel her fire in everything Helen says and does."

Helen is an ordinary person who enjoys babysitting her grandchildren, raising African violets, and meandering down the grocery aisle looking for bargains. But in her enthusiasm, I think she's extraordinary. Her love for God moves her to pause and pray at the site of a beautiful sunset over the ocean—and drives her presence when volunteers are needed for the annual church cleaning. Her passion for the homeless fuels the care and concern she exudes as she pours an extra ladle of meat sauce on spaghetti at the local soup kitchen. Her gratitude glows in the many thank-you notes she deliberately handwrites every month to friends and neighbors.

Eight hundred years before Helen, Francis of Assisi was also consumed with a godly enthusiasm. His love for God burned so ardently that he became a living image of the crucified Christ, branded with the five wounds of the stigmata—something rarely experienced among us today. But, much like my friend Helen, he showed what happens when a person responds to God's longing for us.

Throughout history hundreds of thousands of people have known the fiery passion God has for being in a relationship with us. The sparks from God's longing catch fire in their lives, and by engaging and responding to it, ordinary people like Helen and

Francis become beacons of light who blaze by day and shine brightly by night.

Catching Fire, Becoming Flame: A Guide for Spiritual Transformation gives you the practical tools and time-honored techniques to do the same. It shows you how to respond to God's fiery passion, how to engage it, and, most important, how to be changed by it. Each of its chapters is purposely short and concise, allowing you ample time in one convenient sitting not only to read it, but also to reflect on its questions or practice the presented technique.

This book is designed to be a handy resource for expanding your knowledge and practice of ancient and contemporary spiritual practices. It will fuel your creativity and appreciation for myriad ways to fall in love with God—which, in the end, is what being on fire is all about.

As you practice the spiritual methods of *Catching Fire, Becoming Flame* and make them your own in a distinct way, you will find the flames of godly enthusiasm leaping up in your own life as they do in the lives of all holy people. You will also find yourself gradually transformed into your truest identity: a little Christ—which is what the word *Christian* literally means—sent to lovingly respond to the unmet need or required duty of the present moment.

Albert Haase, OFM
Feast of Pentecost

The

Spark

From

God

AN INTRODUCTION TO THE SPIRITUAL LIFE

God initiates the process of spiritual transformation
by throwing a divine spark into our lives.
God then waits for our response.

CHAPTER 1

A PROCESS OF TRANSFORMATION

■

Sr. Elena was eighty-seven years old, blind, and spent her days in a wheelchair. I didn't notice her when I began preaching the week-long retreat at the retirement home where she resided. But on the afternoon of the second day, she asked someone to push her to me.

"Father, I have a secret to tell you," she said.

I leaned over and she whispered in my ear, "God l-o-n-g-s to turn you into a saint!" Her face lit up as she added, "If you respond to God's yearning, you'll be amazed at what happens."

Though it's been more than two decades since I heard Sr. Elena's secret, I can still feel the ardor and passion that accompanied her revelation. In one short moment, Sr. Elena taught me that God's longing to be in a relationship with us spreads like wildfire in the hearts of people who respond to it. They can't contain what becomes like a fire in the belly, a burning in their bones (see Jeremiah 20:9). No wonder their devotion is memorable and contagious.

Let's take a broad, quick overview at the process God uses in preparing and then setting people on fire with divine love.

A Process

Catching and crackling with the fire of godly enthusiasm is a lifelong *process*. It starts with God throwing a divine spark on the tinder of the heart. I'll describe that spark in greater detail in the next chapter. For now, it's helpful to know that it often comes out of nowhere and can take many different shapes and sizes. It might be an attraction or religious sentiment that grips the heart. It might be an event or situation that stirs your devotion. It could even be a word spoken by a friend, colleague, or relative that gets underneath the skin and stings your conscience.

If we fan the spark to flame and then stoke its fire with spiritual practices, it will ever so gradually transform us into beacons of light for the world. Sometimes it might flare up, shooting its sparks elsewhere as it did with Sr. Elena.

Because this is a gradual, ongoing process, we must resist the temptation to aim for perfection. Perfection is never attained this side of heaven. When we seek perfection, we quickly become discouraged since most of us are burdened by our imperfections, weaknesses, and sins. Discouragement brings us to that slippery slope where we might be tempted to abandon the spiritual journey altogether. And that's what the deadly sin of acedia is all about: throwing water on our smoldering spiritual embers, covering them with dirt, and walking away.

It's more realistic to aim for progress rather than perfection. We daily try to move just one step away from the ego. We daily try to move just one step out of the limelight. We daily try to move closer to those in need.

We also must resist the temptation to look for a single book, program, practice, or guru that will cause spontaneous combustion; there are none. How many times have I been tricked into thinking that by reading the most recent book by a favorite author or practicing the latest spiritual craze, I'll become a saint? A wise spiritual director once said to me, "There's no spiritual microwave oven you can put yourself in and come out sixty seconds later as a saint. You must be willing to jump into the crockpot called your life and simmer a lifetime." Catching fire takes patience and perseverance; it's hard, fatiguing work. It also requires a daily commitment to nurturing and tending the fire once it's been lit.

It's important to remember that the process of catching fire and becoming flame will be different in each person's life. A third temptation we must resist is trying to live another person's process. There is no "cookie cutter" approach to holiness. The spiritual tradition offers us the saints to stir our inspiration, not our strict imitation.

I still remember the day I was so discouraged as a young friar. I had been trying to imitate Saint Francis as perfectly as possible—and I kept falling short. I was seriously considering leaving the Franciscan Order. When I confessed this to my spiritual director, he asked in amazement, "What on earth do you mean?"

I replied, "Saint Francis saw God in all creation. He would walk in the woods, and when he heard the birds chirp, he would bow in adoration of the God who created them. When he came upon wildflowers, he said a prayer of praise for the God who created them. When I walk in the woods, I don't see God anywhere. I just return with bird droppings on my shoulder and poison ivy on my hands!"

My spiritual director wisely counseled me, "Albert, God does not want another Francis of Assisi. He already has one. What God would love to have—and doesn't have just yet—is just one Saint Albert Haase of New Orleans. Find your own path to holiness, follow it, and never apologize for it."

In his 2018 apostolic exhortation, *Rejoice and Be Glad: On the Call to Holiness in Today's World*, Pope Francis makes a similar point: "There are some testimonies that may prove helpful and inspiring, but that we are not meant to copy, for that could even lead us astray from the one specific path that the Lord has in mind for us. The important thing is that each believer discern his or her own path. . . ."[1]

In Community

Paradoxically, our own unique process of catching fire does not occur in a hermetically sealed jar, apart from our roles as spouses, parents, colleagues, and friends. There are no lone rangers or independent contractors when it comes to growing in holiness. We catch fire and become the flame of love for God and others as we live in families and rub shoulders with our friends and colleagues.

A story from the Carmelite tradition hits the nail on the head. One day, a friar was complaining to Saint John of the Cross about a certain member in the community. "I don't know why God put this man in our midst. He's such a troublemaker." Saint John of the Cross quickly replied, "To help us grow in holiness."

Transformation

As God tries to spark our hearts into flame and we actively respond with spiritual practices, we *are transformed*. Note the passive voice. Saint John of the Cross compares this process of transformation to a log catching fire. The heat of the fire initially expels the log's moisture and other inconsistencies, blackens the wood as the fire burns on the log's exterior, and then gradually transforms the log into flame as it burns from within.[2] That's why we can look back some ten or fifteen years, reflect on our lives then and now, and ask with embarrassment, surprise, or disgust, "Who *was* the person who did *that*? How could *that* have been *me*?" This gradual transformation occurs not only on the exterior and cosmetic level of our actions, but also, and more important, on the interior and cardiac level of our thoughts, feelings, and desires.

The Work of the Spirit

Living with a blazing fire does not happen on our own by sheer willpower. As the words *spirit*uality, *spirit*ual life, and *spirit*ual formation suggest, we have to rely upon *the Spirit of God* and divine grace working on us and in us. The Spirit, and the Spirit alone, is the flint for all holiness. The Spirit then also becomes the fuel for our enthusiasm. Without the Spirit, our spiritual lives as Christians flicker out and become cold; with the Spirit, we are sent forth as zealous torches of devotion.

How do I know if the Spirit is setting me on fire? I might think visions and apparitions or growth in other worldly virtues betray the work of the Spirit. That answer couldn't be further from the truth. As the Spirit ignites the embers in my heart, I am driven deeper into this world and into relationships with others. This is how Saint Paul states it: "The fruit of the Spirit is love, joy, peace, patience, kindness, generosity, faithfulness, gentleness, and self-control" (Galatians 5:22–23). The Spirit sets me on fire for this world, not another one.

The Image of Christ

Catching fire is not supposed to be a flash in the pan. And it becomes just that if we do not spend time tending and stoking the fire set by God's spark. It will easily flame out if we do not commit daily, monthly, and yearly to myriad and varied spiritual practices that the Christian tradition offers, and which are discussed in this book. Fire needs tending just as grace needs a response. There is no other way.

As someone responds to the Spirit's action, he or she is ever so gradually transformed into *the image of Christ*. That's the essence of the spiritual life: we are called to become who we profess to be by virtue of our baptism. We are "Christian," which literally means "a little Christ."

The waters of Baptism along with their gift of the Holy Spirit fuel a spiritual transformation that requires a lifetime of surrender. This gradual transformation of our identity is not a mime act, a caricature, or playacting. Rather, as in John of the Cross's log metaphor, the fire of God's love purifies our egos; it ignites our minds, words, wills, and actions so that we can say with Jesus, "Not my will but yours be done" (see Luke 22:42). It is then over time that we reach spiritual maturity, "the full stature of Christ" (Ephesians 4:13). Like Christ, who came "to bring fire to the earth" (Luke 12:49), we challenge institutional religion's insensitivity to the outcast and marginalized by becoming arsonists of divine love and compassion.

Respond to the Unmet Need
or Required Duty of the Present

For I was hungry and
you gave me food, I was
thirsty and you gave me
something to drink, I was
a stranger and you wel-
comed me, I was naked and
you gave me clothing, I was
sick and you took care of
me, I was in prison and you
visited me.

Matthew 25:35–36

As we respond and slowly grow into the image of Christ, our hearts expand, and the Spirit enlarges the circle of our relationships. Our fire cannot be restrained or suppressed in the hermetically sealed container of a single life for the sole purpose of our own personal sanctification. "No one after lighting a lamp puts it under the bushel basket" (Matthew 5:15). That would indeed quench the flame. Rather, through the daily discipline of prayer, the weekly practice of sharing our time, treasures, and talents with others along with attending church services, and the monthly commitment to spiritual practices such as Scripture reading and journaling combined with a yearly retreat, our godly enthusiasm becomes like a wildfire, moving us beyond ourselves, focusing our Christlike lives on others, for others, and with others. It leads us right into the heart of a suffering, needy world where we are *sent to lovingly respond to the unmet need or required duty of the present moment*. As we cook meals, change diapers, and commute back and forth to the office, discovering who we are and how to stoke our godly enthusiasm, we become torchbearers of God's mercy to the hungry, the thirsty, the stranger, the sick, the naked, and the imprisoned. Without a sense of mission, godly enthusiasm fizzles into bogus piety.

I remember myself in my late teens and early twenties as a needy, selfish, egotistical young adult. I often used humor to control people and situations. I still recall attending a party in my sophomore year of college and spending the entire evening desperately trying to get people to laugh so I would be considered the life of the party. Some forty-five years later, through the generosity of God's grace and a commitment to daily prayer and other spiritual practices, I am no longer obsessed with other people's affection and attention. I no longer use humor as a subtle form of manipulation. Something has changed inside of me, and my selfishness and need to control gave way to a decade of missionary service to Catholics in mainland China. I know from my own experience that from her darkness in the wheelchair, Sr. Elena illumined a great truth: you will be amazed at what gradually happens over a lifetime if you respond to God's longing.

God yearns to set us ablaze. As we open ourselves up to this divine love, we discover a fire being ignited and then glowing and sometimes raging in our lives. We experience *the communal process of being transformed by the Spirit of God to the image of Christ sent to lovingly respond to the unmet need or required duty of the present moment.*[3] God's longing and call for this process to begin sometimes come in and through our deepest desires and attractions.

■ REFLECT
1. Fire is one image that captures the intensity of God's yearning to be in a relationship with us. What other images speak to you?
2. Which Pauline fruits of the Spirit are active in your life? Which are inactive?
3. How have other people helped you catch fire?

CHAPTER 2

DESIRE AND SPIRITUAL AWAKENING

∎

While I was being interviewed on a national Catholic talk radio show, Stacey, from Austin, Texas, called into the show.

"Father, I'm a happy stay-at-home mom with two small children. Lately, though, I've been restless and feeling a strange attraction to prayer. But I must be honest: my husband and I are not regular churchgoers. So I'm wondering if I'm just imagining this. And my jobs as a mom and wife don't allow me the freedom to walk away and hide beyond the walls of a monastery. I'm calling to ask your advice. What am I supposed to do?"

I tried my best to show Stacey the special invitation she was being offered.

God's Passionate Invitation to Us

God is always trying to awaken a dormant soul and set it on fire with godly enthusiasm. Our deepest impulses and yearnings for the things of God can be God's way of throwing sparks at us. Religious interests, pious aspirations, and spiritual longings that seemingly come out of nowhere do, in fact, show we have captured divine attention and that God is now trying to capture ours. We desire God because God first desires us. The mere awareness of being attracted to prayer or wanting to make God some part of daily life is the beginning of the process of being transformed. Before that awareness, we are like sleepwalkers. Life is a task-oriented game characterized by flatness, sluggishness, and, sometimes, lackluster monotony. Many are quite content to live this way. Stacey certainly was. She had spent her days with virtually the same routine: bathing the children, entertaining them with trips to the park and zoo, planning the evening meal, and, on weekends, occasionally going to church when it was convenient for her and her family. But now a spiritual spark is touching and scorching her heart. She is becoming restless. And without her even knowing it right now, her phone call for advice is the beginning of her response to God. Sooner or later we all discover that restlessness comes into our lives for a profound purpose: so that we may begin a relationship with God. This is the awakening.

The divine spark of the Holy Spirit—the flint and flame of godly enthusiasm—triggers the awakening. Without it, we would be rubbing two sticks together in the pouring rain.

> Wake up from your sleep, Climb out of your coffins; Christ will show you the light!
>
> Ephesians 5:14, MSG

God's spark can find us in any situation, circumstance, or event. Some experiences are powerfully positive: a weekend retreat, the birth of a child, an uplifting worship service, a heart-to-heart conversation with a trusted friend, someone's profession of love for us, or the sight of a beautiful sunset. Sometimes the catalyst is painful: a loved one's death, the diagnosis of a disease, the loss of a home in a natural disaster, or being laid off from work. In either case, this experience of grace is unique to each person and tailored to his or her season and situation. The circumstances are limitless since nothing is impossible with God (see Luke 1:37).

Two of the most formative years of my life were spent when I was a boarder in a Franciscan high school seminary in Cincinnati. At the age of fifteen, while wanting to improve my handball game and hone my public speaking skills for a state speech contest, I began feeling an attraction and magnetic pull to the chapel for personal prayer. I tried my best to squelch those feelings because I didn't understand what they meant, and I certainly didn't want my classmates to think I was abandoning handball for a higher power. I remember going to see Fr. Murray and sheepishly asking about them. With a wisdom born from his own experience, he matter-of-factly replied, "That's God tugging at your heart and looking for some company. Why don't you oblige him sometimes?"

The awakening is God's invitation to a relationship. But it still requires our response. God will never force or put pressure upon us; with utmost respect for human free will, God can only invite us, encourage us, nudge us, and entice us. God tugs at the heart. And God does so through spiritual desires and longings that are placed deep within us. Stacey learned that in her own life. It's ultimately up to us to do something about them, to respond to God's generous bidding to be in a relationship with us.

Human Hesitations

If we choose to throw cold water on the kindling and not respond, God is forced to wait again and use another situation or event to spark us into flame.

Two misconceptions might keep us from responding to God's invitation. One resembles Stacey's initial insinuation that, not being a regular churchgoer, she was somehow unworthy, as if it was too late for her to connect with God.

It is never too late to begin fanning the flames. God's patience and generosity are magnanimous. That's why spiritual thoughts or feelings suddenly like flying sparks arise out of nowhere and keep recurring. They are indications of God's insistent determination to have a relationship with us. Jesus's parable of the workers in the vineyard (see Matthew 20:1–16) speaks to this. A landowner goes out at various hours and hires day laborers to work in his vineyard. At the end of the day, when the landowner pays them, the laborers who worked only an hour received the same per diem as those hired at the beginning of the day. Jesus does not say the late hires received a full day's pay because they worked hard and gave it their all but because the landowner was "generous" (see verse 15).

A significant lesson of that parable is that our time and God's patience never run out. The important thing is not *when* we begin to get serious about responding to God's invitation, but *that* we begin. It makes no difference whether you are fifteen years old as I was or in your forties as was the Carmelite mystic Teresa of Avila. And the moment we respond, we lose any apparent disadvantage that our tardiness, laziness, or lack of previous motivation might have imposed. A simple yes to God—no matter when it is spoken—fans the spark of godly enthusiasm and begins the process of our being transformed into the image of Christ.

Stacey's phone call also suggested another misconception that might keep us from responding to God's invitation: the supposition that a relationship with God requires the abandonment of all spousal responsibilities, parental duties, and employment obligations. As Stacey put it, "And my jobs as a mom and wife don't allow me the freedom to walk away and hide beyond the walls of a monastery." Nothing could be further from the truth. The wonderful thing about God's invitation is that we can accept it right where we are. Throughout history people have done so as they went to school, raised a family, or went to the office to earn a paycheck. That's part of the contagion of godly enthusiasm and the paradox of catching fire and becoming flame: the extraordinary occurs right in the midst of the ordinary; the mystical and marvelous are found amid the monotonous and mundane.

■ REFLECT

1. Reflect and pray over the famous words of St. Augustine: "You have made us for yourself, O Lord, and our hearts are restless until they rest in you."[4] What does this say about the attractions and desires of your heart? Which ones speak of God's invitation to you?

2. When have you experienced a spiritual awakening? Did you respond immediately, or did you hesitate to respond? Why?

3. What misconceptions might be hindering you from responding to God's invitation to a deeper relationship?

CHAPTER 3

THE THREE STAGES
OF THE SPIRITUAL JOURNEY

■

As I crisscross the country giving workshops on the spiritual life, I am often asked to give more details about the process of transformation by the Spirit of God. How do I begin to respond to God's desire to have a relationship with me? What does the process of spiritual transformation look like? How do I know if it is happening to me? These are important questions, and our rich spiritual tradition not only answers them but also offers some sage advice to people who want to burn with godly enthusiasm.

If you are willing to respond to God's invitation that comes through an awakening, you will suddenly find yourself walking along what's been called the threefold path or the threefold way. Rather than being distinct, discrete stages, these three transformative stages to the spiritual life are more like processes, movements, or actions that occur at various times and at various and deepening levels of our lives.

The Stage of Purgation

Once awakened and ready to respond, we are like a spark that needs help to become something greater. During this initial stage of transformation, called *purgation*, we arrange the kindling and wood by deliberately fostering attitudes and actions that reflect a person who is serious about catching fire. The tasks of this first stage are characterized by the acronym CPR: community, prayer, and repentance.

Community: The English idiom "Birds of a feather flock together," speaks to the first task of the purgative stage. We begin by building bonds of support with a regular church community so that we are surrounded by other people who are similarly on fire—or at least smoldering! Jesus himself modeled the importance of community with the call of the twelve disciples; the early church lived out its ramifications in a practical way.

Now the whole group of those who believed were of one heart and soul, and no one claimed private ownership of any possessions, but everything they owned was held in common. With great power the apostles gave their testimony to the resurrection of the Lord Jesus, and great grace was upon them all. There was not a needy person among them, for as many as owned lands or houses sold them and brought the proceeds of what was sold. They laid it at the apostles' feet, and it was distributed to each as any had need.

Acts 4:32–35

As I mentioned in chapter 1, spiritual transformation is not meant to be a solitary, individual affair; nor is it done in isolation from the world. It stretches the heart beyond the ego— "from me to thee," as a wise spiritual director once told me. Being transformed into the image of Christ involves selfless love and service. This is learned within a community of flesh-and-blood believers who "wash each other's feet," learn to forgive each other, celebrate life events as sacramental moments, and welcome to their table the poor, the sinner, and the marginalized. Christianity without community is a caricature.

Prayer: CPR includes the commitment to daily prayer. What is critical is not *how* we pray, but *that* we pray for an amount of time appropriate for our commitments and schedules. For some, the most helpful form of prayer will be a conversation at the same time every day, when we convey to God our thoughts and feelings and then wait in silence for God to respond. That's what I did at age fifteen when I intentionally started praying for twenty minutes every day. This form of prayer can conveniently take place on the bus or a commuter train. Others might find more conducive to their temperament a simple and structured pattern, like repeating traditional prayers while using a rosary or repeating the Jesus Prayer ("Jesus, Son of David, have mercy on me, a sinner"). Still others might turn to Scripture. One of the first challenges in the process of spiritual transformation is discovering the prayer techniques that fan the flame and make us receptive to God's continual presence throughout the day. I encourage people initially to try different and varied prayer techniques, until they happen upon the ones that are comfortable and helpful for them.

Repentance: The final task of purgation's CPR is repentance, which involves purging ourselves of the deliberate sins that we nonchalantly commit; it is about removing the moisture that hinders us from catching fire. We choose to start moving out of the shadows and darkness where we have been content to live. We make an examination of conscience, take an inventory of our lives, and take conscious steps toward moral integration. The Christian values that we profess with our lips become the Christian values that we intentionally put into practice: forgiveness involves letting go of grudges; compassion includes deepening our sensitivity to the marginalized; kindness means dying to selfish desires. Repentance and conversion—from the Greek word *metanoia*, meaning "to turn around"—demand changing the orientation of our daily lives.

The Stage of Illumination

Over time, if we are faithful to CPR, we will perceive the Spirit of God working in our lives. That awareness—of the Spirit's interior work—is a typical indication of the second stage or process of the spiritual journey, *illumination.*

Unlike the stage of purgation, which can be seen exteriorly, this stage is internal and, as the name suggests, is characterized by light and enlightenment. As the Spirit's spark becomes a flame and then matures into a fire, we begin to see how Christian beliefs and values make sense. We take on an intuitive understanding and wisdom of the things of God. The commitments to community and prayer, once requiring the effort needed for any discipline, become more natural and are the ways by which we express our deepening enthusiasm and love for God.

It is in this stage that we discover the great insight: God is closer to us than we have ever thought or imagined. Indeed, there is nothing to get in the spiritual life because we already have it. We simply need to grow in deeper awareness of what we already have, namely, the presence of God that surrounds us like the air we breathe and dwells within us. This insight glows hot in the illuminative stage.

Trustful surrender characterizes the illuminative stage, as Christians give themselves over to the action of the Holy Spirit. While the stage of purgation is active, the stage of illumination is more receptive; we allow something to be done to us. This receptive stance is strengthened by the emotional sense of being led by Someone bigger than our own egos. The purgative stage's guilt for past sin is now replaced by the illuminative stage's sorrow for having wasted so much time. Selfless acts become second nature as we are shaped, molded, and prodded along by the Spirit of God. During this second process, God's grace is doing most of the work and action.

The Stage of Union

Fidelity to the CPR purgative practices and the trustful surrender characteristic of the illuminative stage gradually come to fruition in the third stage, called *union*. As awakening can be likened to a spark landing on ripe kindling, purgation to fanning the flame, and illumination to catching fire, union is likened to the experience of becoming a torch with a fire blazing from within. At this stage, we not only know but also experience union with God and God's will: so united are we to God that God's desires are our desires.

At this stage, in a vivid and obvious way, we do not simply *live* the Christian life but are in fact *being* and *acting* as little Christs. Here the fire is stoked with the wisdom of the Beatitudes, and we crackle with missional energy and passion for the loving service of others. Like Christ and with Christ, we are ablaze and sent by God as a coworker for the kingdom (see Colossians 4:11).

Two final thoughts regarding the threefold path are helpful to remember. First, it is not neatly and clearly delineated. The three stages or processes are fluid as divine grace works upon human nature. We could be experiencing all three stages at the same time: the memory could be experiencing an awakening, while the intellect and what it is thinking are in the illuminative stage and the will with its desires is working on purgative practices. This means we don't complete the homework of one stage and automatically graduate to the next stage. That's why I remind people that it is a misguided use of time to try and track where they are. The Spirit of God is ultimately in charge of the entire process, and divine grace is often more complicated and messier—and sometimes simpler—than these three delineated stages might suggest.

Second, though the threefold path is firmly grounded in the history of Christian spirituality, God is not bound by it. Grace is always unpredictable and what we sometimes are expecting, does not happen—or happens at an earlier or later stage. Some people experience a spontaneous combustion and live in the unitive stage at an early age while others spend a lifetime plodding along with the CPR of the purgative stage. We need to keep in mind that spiritual transformation is about progress, not perfection, and God is ultimately in charge. As someone in spiritual direction once said to me, "I am where I am because this is where God wants me to be. When God wants me to become flame, grace will come into my life and set me ablaze. Until then, my task is simply to be faithful and fan any spark God sends my way."

■ REFLECT

1. How are you living out the purgative practices of community, prayer, and repentance in your daily life right now? Which of the three needs greater attention?

2. Where is the Holy Spirit currently working in your life? How might your actions and attitudes hinder the Spirit's guidance?

3. What is God's will and desire for you?

CHAPTER 4

IMPERFECTIONS VERSUS SINS

■

James was stuck in discouragement and regret.

"Once again, my short fuse was just too short. I came home the other day tired from work. The kids wanted some attention and asked me to play with them. Instead of giving them five minutes of my time, which would have more than satisfied them, I just snapped. I raised my voice and told them I had been working all day and just needed some time to relax. This happens at least once or twice a month, and every time it does, I feel terrible afterward. I've been working so hard on my relationship with God and then something like this happens, and I realize I am a total failure. Where have I gone wrong?"

Listening to James, I leaned back in my chair and momentarily thought how we struggle with imperfections—and sin!

Imperfections and Weaknesses

All of us, like James, struggle with imperfections and weaknesses such as impatience and anger. Before we accept God's invitation to enter a relationship, we instinctively give in to them in a variety of situations without much thought or reflection. But after we respond to the initial invitation and then become intentional about an ongoing relationship with God, something slowly changes in us.

Many people are surprised to discover that the more they are willing to deliberately fan God's spark of grace, the more their weaknesses and sins are illumined. Indeed, growth in the spiritual life is growth in the awareness of the darkness in my life. This should never, ever be a source of discouragement. This awareness leads to the recognition that I need a savior and that catching fire and becoming flame are all actions of the grace of God.

Awareness is a powerful tool in the ongoing process of spiritual transformation. Simply becoming aware of our ongoing struggles is the beginning of being set free from them. Awareness is not supposed to load us down with guilt; instead, it should bolster us by making us sensitive and vigilant, helping us to reconsider and short-circuit spontaneous reactions and bad habits. Coming to an awareness of a weakness as James did is always a step forward, not backward.

We are now able to do something that, before, we never could have done as well: take a hard, honest look at our imperfections and weaknesses. We ask ourselves: in what areas of life do we need God's grace and the light of Christ?

The Childhood Trigger

Imperfections, weaknesses, flaws, defects, failings, and short-comings are part and parcel of the human condition. No one is perfect; in some areas we all lack maturity. These areas are often hooked to real or perceived childhood deprivations. In an adult, childhood deficiencies, whether real or imagined, may become predilections, inclinations, fixations, preoccupations, compulsions, infatuations, and sometimes addictions.

Here are some examples: A man raised in a family that struggled financially may grow up to become a hoarder and be obsessive about money and possessions; he may also be prone to envy what others have. A girl raised in an abusive family might grow up always looking for ways to feel accepted and loved; she might become a compulsive shopper or develop a chemical addiction to ease the emotional pain of her childhood. A "middle child" who felt neglected in youth might become preoccupied with gaining people's attention and admiration.

Such knee-jerk reactions form the heart of our imperfections and weaknesses. We do not consciously or deliberately choose them. They gradually become bad habits or predictable, spontaneous reactions that disappoint our best selves. That's why awareness is the first critical step in overcoming them and being freed from them.

Such fixations and compulsions need to be admitted and brought into the light. Once we become aware of our preoccupations and compulsions, we look for the emotional "trigger": the childhood memory, feeling, event, or deficiency that it serves, caters to, and appeases. We need to disengage the trigger to short-circuit the fixation or addiction. Disengaging the trigger is no easy task, and we can rarely do so on our own.

Practicing the prayer of inner healing that I'll discuss in chapter 29 is a helpful start. Twelve-step support groups have a history of helping people live with addictive personalities. Counseling or psychotherapy coupled with spiritual direction is also useful in deepening the awareness of the trigger as well as its effects upon us.

Don't allow guilt to gobble you up. Discouragement and shame over your imperfections and weaknesses waste a lot of emotional energy. They do not offer any positive consequences. Awareness of a personal weakness ideally leads to action, not simply to a begrudging apology or a deflated sense of being a failure.

The Difference between Impulse and Sin

Sin is something very different from these knee-jerk impulses or emotional triggers that we often act upon without reflection. Sin is a conscious and deliberate *choice*. It is a firm decision—a freely chosen act of the will—to be self-centered, thus dousing the fire of godly enthusiasm and interrupting the transformation into the image of Christ.

Sometimes we consistently choose a certain sin, and it becomes a bad habit: think of someone who consistently makes a choice for alcohol, food, or shopping that backfires into a full-blown addiction. What started as a willful decision becomes over time a chain of slavery that is no longer freely chosen. That's why sins can be more dangerous than we sometimes think.

Deliberately chosen sinful actions are typically commentaries and variations on the seven deadly sins: pride, anger, envy, lust, gluttony, greed, and acedia (the dissatisfaction and discouragement with our spiritual life that lead us to definitively end our relationship with God). These seven deadly sins feed our overemotional investment in:

- self-concern (pride);
- self-image (pride, anger, envy);
- self-gratification (lust, greed, gluttony, acedia);
- self-preservation (greed).

We can become so wrapped up in our achievements and accomplishments that we begin to think we are self-made individuals. We obsess over what people think of us and begin treating those who dislike us as enemies. Without hesitation, we allow our desires to rule and make decisions about how we should act. We make sure we never run out of food, possessions, and money. Paul refers to the actions associated with these self-centered concerns as the "works of the flesh" (see Galatians 5:19–21).

I also like to think of sin in terms of an acronym whose letters stand for those acts when the ego takes over control, assumes total supremacy, and "eases God out" of one's life. Our godly enthusiasm is then quickly replaced with a hunkered-down self-centeredness.

But there is more to sin than acts of commission. The ego also throws its weight around with sins of omission. Closely aligned to imperfections and weaknesses, these are deliberately chosen acts that ignore the opportunity to express what Paul calls the "fruit of the

Spirit": love, joy, peace, patience, kindness, generosity, faithfulness, gentleness, and self-control (see Galatians 5:22–23). Banking the fire of godly enthusiasm is not just about stopping certain sinful actions; it is also about practicing certain virtuous actions:

- Acts of generosity shortchange greed;
- self-control puts gluttony on a diet;
- chastity gives lust a cold shower;
- patience tempers anger;
- humble service knocks pride off the pedestal;
- perseverance pulls acedia up from the couch;
- self-acceptance and trust in God's providence put an end to envy.

Such virtuous acts challenge us to overcome the emotional fixation with self-concern, self-image, self-gratification, and self-preservation.

There is also a corporate dimension to sin. Some individuals create and promote systems, processes, attitudes, and mentalities that are antithetical to the most basic Christian principles. Obvious examples are unjust political regimes or racist organizations such as the Ku Klux Klan and the Proud Boys. Closer to home are companies that have unethical practices of hiring and promotion or firms that are dishonest and turn a blind eye to governmental laws and municipal regulations. To the

A man had a fig tree planted in his vineyard; and he came looking for fruit on it and found none. So he said to the gardener, "See here! For three years I have come looking for fruit on this fig tree, and still I find none. Cut it down! Why should it be wasting the soil?" He replied, "Sir, let it alone for one more year, until I dig around it and put manure on it. If it bears fruit next year, well and good; but if not, you can cut it down."

Luke 13:6–9

extent that we participate in such organizations and do not actively work for their transformation, we are coconspirators, collaborators, and accomplices to corporate sin.

Though the four Gospels record a few passing incidents when Jesus uses the word *sin* (see Matthew 5:29; Mark 3:29 and its parallels; John 8:7; 8:34; 8:46; 16:9), they do not give us a clear understanding of what he means by the term. Six of Jesus's parables, however, suggest that he equates sin with a flat refusal to change and grow, to forgive and be compassionate.

Pause for a moment and ask yourself the following questions:

- How willing and flexible am I to change my attitudes and behaviors that I know in my heart go against the teachings of Jesus?
- How often do I deliberately let go of a grudge or hurt and embrace the person who betrayed me?
- When do I ignore the beggar on the street or retreat from those marginalized by the church and society?

Believe it or not, you have just examined your conscience based upon Jesus's understanding of sin found in his parables. The parables of the sower (Mark 4:3–8) and the barren fig tree (Luke 13:6–9) highlight the importance of being productive and bearing fruit; hence, they speak to the need to change attitudes and behaviors—and be transformed. The parable of the unforgiving servant (Matthew 18:23– 35) reminds us of the need to forgive as we have been forgiven. The parables of the good Samaritan (Luke 10:30–37), the rich man and Lazarus (Luke 16:19–31), and the judgment of the nations (Matthew 25:31–46) all illustrate the importance of love, compassion, and a generous heart. These parables suggest that Jesus understands sin as a deliberate resistance to the Spirit's transformation, a direct refusal to catch fire. It has less to do with the violation of a law.

Many people, unfortunately, narrowly define sin as simply breaking commandments and violating rules and regulations. As you can hopefully now see, Jesus understands it as a deeper, more fundamental stance and decision: an iron-willed, obstinate resistance to catching fire and fanning the flames of godly enthusiasm, a stubborn refusal to be transformed by grace into the image of Christ.

The Leper's Prayer

The awareness of the origin of our weaknesses and the recognition of our deliberately chosen sins sometimes can leave us feeling not only discouraged but also like modern-day lepers in search of healing. When I feel consumed by feelings of failure or guilt, I turn to the Leper's Prayer I wrote a few years ago:

Lord Jesus,
I come before you
Burdened by my obsessive desires,
Bruised by my selfish choices,
And broken by my sinfulness.
Like a modern-day leper,
I feel unwanted, unclean, and untouchable—to myself and others.
I am imprisoned by my body
And scarred by my weaknesses and imperfections.
A desperate plea oozes through my open sores:
Stretch forth the healing hand of your love.
Secure for me what I lacked in my childhood.
Shatter the shame of my sin with your compassion and understanding.
Restore me to the community
Of those you have chosen for everlasting life and eternal salvation.

Then filled with gratitude and thanksgiving,
I will clap,
Dance,
And shout your praises
Until the day I stand face-to-face before your Father
Alongside those marked with the sign of faith.
I ask this
In your name.
Amen.

■ REFLECT

1. What are your weaknesses and bad habits? What childhood memory, event, or experience might have given birth to each of them?

2. How does awareness of your weaknesses and imperfections affect your spiritual journey? How can you change your life in light of that awareness?

3. How does Jesus's understanding of sin challenge your own understanding of sin? Under what circumstances do you deliberately resist and refuse the Spirit's transformation?

CHAPTER 5

BREAKING BAD HABITS

∎

Before we are spiritually awakened and begin fanning the flame of godly enthusiasm in our lives, we are like sleepwalkers. We go through life unaware of the many ways in which we subvert the transformative grace of the Spirit. However, once we begin walking the threefold path and get serious about CPR—connecting to a community, praying daily, and making a conscious effort to repent from deliberate sin—we quickly discover that our moral lives are a lot messier than we had ever imagined.

Still, saying no to deliberate sin can be a lot easier than breaking the bad habits in which many of us are entrenched. Our misuse of food, alcohol, gambling, sexual desires, and shopping, along with obsessions about violence, love, money, anger, work, or our appearance, often hinder our loving response to the unmet need or required duty of the present moment. Many of these obsessions have become bad habits that need to be recognized, admitted, and broken.

Steps to Freedom

Breaking a bad habit is not an easy task. But it's not impossible. It begins with awareness—the conscious recognition and realization that we constantly react in the same unacceptable way to certain situations or thoughts.

Writing is not my preferred medium of communication. I think of myself as a preacher, not a writer. So when I am working on a writing project, I allow my personality to change from an outgoing, affable person who is quick to belly laugh to an intense person, consumed with my thoughts and ideas, irritable, and a bit standoffish. I was never aware of this until a friend called to invite me out to dinner and said, "Bring the preacher—but please, leave the writer at home. I want to have a relaxing meal." Something clicked inside me as I suddenly became aware that writing was the trigger that sparked a personality change in me.

Once we realize we have a bad habit, it's wise to monitor ourselves. The following questions can be helpful: When am I most vulnerable to reacting with the unacceptable behavior? What situations or circumstances tempt me to act in a reactive way, without reflective consideration? This kind of awareness and monitoring can help sensitize us to the emotional trigger that provokes the behavior.

Once we know what our bad habits are and what triggers them, we need to ask if we really want to change them. To break a bad habit demands the focused, attentive energy of willpower. If we say we "should" change this behavior, we are still only at the awareness stage. If we say we "want" to change this behavior, we are probably ready to continue.

We often treat our bad habits as friends even though they bring out the worst in us. And sometimes they are the medication we self-prescribe to avoid some painful thought or its accompanying emotion. Ever notice how temptations toward compulsive activity such as overeating, binge drinking, inappropriate sexual activity, gambling, or shopping suddenly emerge when you find yourself in a stressful or emotionally charged situation? That awareness reveals your medication of choice. So we need to give ourselves time to grieve the loss of these ill-suited friends as we struggle with the feelings and emotions that we previously did not allow ourselves to fully experience.

Once we have adequately grieved the loss of the habit, we can actively, consciously, and deliberately change and replace the unacceptable behavior with another behavior. Experts tell us that the new behavior must be willfully chosen twenty-one *consecutive* times before a new habit is formed firmly in its place. Think about that for a moment, and how long that will take in your own life. In the case of a false start, where we choose the good behavior for only ten or fifteen times and then allow the unacceptable behavior to return, we need to start again from scratch, counting twenty-one consecutive decisions for the new behavior.

We will initially experience life in a different way as we actively short-circuit the trigger of the habit. Especially in the case of addictions, counseling or psychotherapy along with membership in a twelve-step support group can be helpful in dealing with our new lifestyle and behaviors.

The Mind of Christ

The fourth-century desert tradition of Christianity offers a helpful insight that augments this conscious change of behavior. The early desert fathers and mothers believed that what we think about plays an important role in our spiritual lives. Thoughts matter. Disreputable thoughts create desires that fuel the passions of the seven deadly sins, which often get played out in action.

Thoughts ➔ Desires ➔ Passions ➔ Action

For example:
- We might think that some particular possession will make us happy. Our desire for it fuels our passion for getting it and keeping it. This can then play out in the sin of thievery or selfishness or greed.
- We might feel an attraction to a particular person. We begin to desire the person. And this can lead to the passion of lust, which can be acted upon in a variety of ways.

- Or let's say a person whom we struggle to get along with says an unkind word. We want to get revenge. This desire fuels the passion of anger, which could be expressed with a retaliatory word or action.

Finally, beloved, whatever is true, whatever is honorable, whatever is just, whatever is pure, whatever is pleasing, whatever is commendable, if there is any excellence and if there is anything worthy of praise, think about these things.

Philippians 4:8

The desert Christians encourage us to replace thoughts that could potentially lead to sinful behavior with *different* sorts of thoughts. This was certainly how Jesus himself taught: "You have heard that it was said, 'You shall love your neighbor and hate your enemy.' But I say to you, Love your enemies and pray for those who persecute you" (Matthew 5:43–44). A change of thinking can help lead to a change of behavior.

That's how the desert tradition interprets Paul's injunction to dwell on certain thoughts (Philippians 4:8) and to be transformed "by the renewing of your minds" (Romans 12:2; see also Romans 8:6; Philippians 2:5); it can lead to having "the mind of Christ" (1 Corinthians 2:16). We will probably never know for sure what the mind of Christ fully contains, but between the desert Christians and St. Paul, this is some pretty sure advice! Thoughts both affect and effect our actions.

This practice has helped me deal with my own harsh reactions toward others. Over the years I've discovered that I have judgmental attitudes rooted in the belief that life is a race and other people are competitors trying to get ahead of me. I used to do all I could to maintain my pace and my leading place in that race. Shifting the metaphor for life from a race to a family affair is slowly changing the way I look at people and respond to them. Competitors have now become my brothers and sisters whom I struggle to care for, love, and forgive.

In each of our lives, bad habits can be changed by following a simple process of becoming aware of, monitoring, grieving, and replacing the unacceptable behavior. Changing our thinking helps to strengthen a new behavior and facilitates the Spirit's transformative work in our lives.

■ REFLECT

1. How do your bad habits and unacceptable behaviors subvert the transformative work of the Spirit?

2. Ponder one of your inappropriate actions or sinful behaviors. What's the originating thought or emotional situation that gives birth to the desire to act upon it?

3. What specific thoughts will change your inappropriate action or sinful behavior pondered in reflection question 2? How will you remember these thoughts?

CHAPTER 6

THE LIVING FLAME OF LOVE

■

Two years after the release of the first edition of this book, I received an email from a man in Ottawa, Canada. He wrote:

> Dear Father,
> I attended the viewing of your DVDs *Catching Fire, Becoming Flame* and *Keeping the Fire Alive*, which my parish offered as an adult faith formation program. Afterwards, I decided to buy your book and read it. I like it a lot! Thanks so much for writing it.
> I've returned to the chapter on breaking bad habits time and again. I'm also working on my CPR and I'm finding that very helpful. I'm using some of the prayer practices you mention in the book. So much peace has returned to my life. And I feel like I'm making a lot of progress in my relationship with God. Thanks so very much!
> Gratefully, William

I've received countless similar emails about this book. Every time I receive one, I am reminded of what was glaringly missing from its first edition. Consequently, I fear I gave a false impression about spiritual transformation. In my desire to offer ways to fan God's spark into the flame of godly enthusiasm, I failed to mention explicitly the surest sign of God's spark and the definitive indication of catching fire.

A New Commandment

The Pharisees were pious Jews who developed a rule-oriented spirituality based upon the Torah and its oral interpretation. They wanted to shape a person's actions through obedience to dos and don'ts. The tithing of herbs (see Matthew 23:23; Luke 11:42), the wearing of conspicuous phylacteries and tassels (see Matthew 23:5), the keen attention to ritual purity (see Mark 7:1–4), fasting (see Matthew 9:14), and meticulous distinctions in oaths (see Matthew 23:16–18) were all practices they hoped would set people on fire with godly enthusiasm. The problem was: their strategy didn't work. These spiritual practices only scorched the surface and ultimately became "heavy burdens" placed upon people's shoulders (see Matthew 23:4).

Jesus's understanding of piety wasn't hooked to a rule-based spirituality. Knowing such an emphasis upon externals sparks only fanaticism, not fire, Jesus placed the hearth of spirituality in the heart because that was the source of a person's actions (see Matthew 15:17–20).

Love raged and crackled in Jesus's hearth. Its sparks shot into the lives of women and children as well as public sinners, the marginalized, and outcasts of his day. It stoked his parables about mercy and compassion as well as his teachings about stopping the cycle of violence and turning the other cheek, doing good to our enemies, and forgiving without limitations. It blazed in his final act of laying down his life for his friends.

Jesus ignited this very fire in his disciples. Summarizing the Torah and prophets in the command to love God and neighbor (see Matthew 22:34–40), he passed the torch to the next generation: "I give you a new commandment, that you love one another. Just as I have loved you, you also should love one another. By this everyone will know that you are my disciples, if you have love for one another" (John 13:34–35).

The First Letter of John bluntly equates this new commandment with the fire of godly enthusiasm: "Beloved, let us love one another, because love is from God; everyone who loves is born of God and knows God. Whoever does not love does not know God, for God is love. . . . Those who say, 'I love God,' and hate their brothers and sisters, are liars; for those who do not love a brother or sister whom they have seen, cannot love God whom they have not seen. The commandment we have from him is this: those who love God must love their brothers and sisters also" (1 John 4:7–8, 20–21).

Saint Paul's Understanding of Love

Love never gives up.
Love cares more for others than for self.
Love doesn't want what it doesn't have.
Love doesn't strut,
Doesn't have a swelled head,
Doesn't force itself on others,
Isn't always "me first,"
Doesn't fly off the handle,
Doesn't keep score of the sins of others,
Doesn't revel when others grovel,
Takes pleasure in the flowering of truth,
Puts up with anything,
Trusts God always,
Always looks for the best,
Never looks back,
But keeps going to the end.

1 Corinthians 13:4–7, MSG

Love is the surest sign of God's spark and the definitive indication of catching fire; it is the one and only goal of spiritual transformation. But it is sorely misunderstood. Many believe it to be an emotional connection like infatuation or romantic love—but how can we feel that for people who have betrayed us or whom we consider our enemies? Yet Jesus makes clear that these people also are meant to be loved (see Matthew 5:44–48).

Saint Paul gives us a keen insight into the nature of Christian love. It is not a supersized feeling or gushing emotion. To the Corinthian community that was torn by factions vying for a sense of superiority and prestige, he firmly stated that love must be the basic and preeminent foundation of any person or community claiming to have spiritual gifts. Without love, "I am a resounding gong or a clashing cymbal . . . I am nothing . . . I gain nothing" (1 Corinthians 13:1–3). Highlighting the dynamism of his understanding of love, the Apostle to the Gentiles uses fifteen verbs that are translated as adjectives in English. They point to the intentional dedication and willful commitment he understands love to be. Let's revisit them.

- Love is patient (verse 4). It perseveres, persists, and is tenacious in relationships. It is tolerant and even-tempered. It does not devolve into irritation, frustration, or annoyance.
- Love is kind (verse 4). It is selfless, never selfish. It is the expression of care, concern, and consideration even to those whom I think are unworthy. It is affectionate, altruistic, and attentive.
- Love is not jealous (verse 4). It never gets caught in the game of comparing the gifts and abilities of others with myself. It is never resentful or bitter or covetous. It celebrates the other person with his or her unique talents.
- Love is not pompous; it is not inflated (verse 4). It does not allow a sense of entitlement to dominate others. It is not domineering, overbearing, or condescending. It welcomes everyone as brothers and sisters and considers them as equals in its eyes.
- Love is not rude (verse 5). It is not ill-mannered, impolite, or discourteous. It maintains a polite, civil attitude toward everyone.
- Love does not seek its own interests (verse 5). It has a generous heart and open hands. It is never selfish, greedy, or clingy.

- Love is not quick-tempered (verse 5). It is not abrasive or hurtful. It never moves another to bitter tears.
- Love does not brood over injury (verse 5). It does not tolerate self-pity. It moves beyond a bruised ego.
- Love does not rejoice over wrongdoing but rejoices with the truth (verse 6). It speaks the truth with kindness and sensitivity. It does not deny the facts. It is honest.
- Love bears all things, believes all things, hopes all things, endures all things (verse 7). While honoring my hurts, sorrows, and injuries, it continues to sustain and support those who have treated me unjustly. It embraces compassion and understanding.

As the Spirit transforms us into the image of Christ, our hearts expand and begin burning with a commitment, dedication, and devotion to others. This is Christian love according to Saint Paul. Christian love crackles and sizzles in every selfless act done exclusively for the benefit of another. It is inclusive, uplifting, and freeing. It blazes in the hospitable heart that never turns its back on the world.

When people like William email me and mention that they are making progress in their relationship with God, I suspect they mean they are responding to God's spark of the awakening and finding it satisfying as they work on the purgative stage's CPR. Being surrounded by like-minded people, developing a daily prayer life, and becoming serious about changing one's life are wonderful boosts; they certainly make us feel like we are growing spiritually. But such actions, like the Pharisees', only scorch the surface if our hearts are not expanding and becoming more tender, sensitive, and compassionate. Real progress in spiritual transformation is measured by the size of our hearts and whether they are blazing with an enthusiasm for God expressed in selfless acts for others. Love and love alone is what catching fire and becoming flame are all about.

■ REFLECT

1. What rules govern your own spirituality and approach to spiritual transformation? How do these rules expand the size of your heart and help you fall in love with God and neighbor?

2. What situations in your life give rise to the tension between obeying laws and loving selflessly? How do you resolve this tension and justify your actions?

3. What challenges does Saint Paul's description of love present to you? How do you overcome them?

Kindling

BASIC SPIRITUAL CONCEPTS

*Certain attitudes coupled with an awareness of
basic spiritual principles provide excellent kindling
for the spark from God to catch flame in our lives.*

CHAPTER 7

DOES YOUR GOD LOVE YOU?

■

Born of practicing Jews, Jesus would have been raised as a pious Jew. He was taught the Torah and how to interpret it. He was also taught the "tradition of the elders" (see Matthew 15:2; Mark 7:13) that circumscribed the religious practice of his day and determined whether a person was in good standing with the God of Abraham, Isaac, and Jacob. Taught to love God with his whole heart, soul, strength, and mind, he would have also learned that one should preserve a reverential fear and distance from this God.

But somewhere along the line, a spark caught fire in Jesus.

The image of God as Abba—Father—was the fire crackling in the soul of Jesus. Everything that Jesus taught and did radiated from it: his outreach to the marginalized, his table fellowship with sinners, and his parables about love, forgiveness, and generosity were all sparks shooting from his insight that God was an amazingly close and intimate Father.

A healthy image of God can focus our own godly enthusiasm. It provides excellent kindling not only for the transformative process of the Holy Spirit, but also for our loving response to the unmet need or required duty of the present moment.

Unhealthy images of God, on the other hand, typically elicit unhealthy behavior. To think of God as a dictator, warden, or traffic cop will keep us self-conscious and hiding in the bushes, cowering in fear. An image of God as an amorphous energy force will keep our relationship with God distant, uninspiring, and impersonal. Viewing God as Santa Claus makes us focus on our wants, and imagining God as a divine puppeteer keeps us hoping that the right strings are pulled. Each of these images of God fails to enkindle the fire that challenges us to loving service of our neighbors.

No saint better exemplifies the transformative power of one's image of God than Thérèse of Lisieux. Realizing that holiness, in the tradition of the great spiritual giants who had lived before her, was beyond her grasp, she began to practice her "way of spiritual childhood." She daily recognized her nothingness, confidently abandoned herself to God, and expected God to give her everything she needed, just as children expect everything from their parents. Despite her debilitating tuberculosis and the personality clashes inherent in her convent setting, this practice of enthusiastic trust challenged her to renounce all worry and live the carefree life of a child. She described her spirituality of spiritual childhood to one of the sisters like this: "It means not to attribute to ourselves the virtues we practice, not to believe that we are capable of anything, but to acknowledge that it is the good Lord who has placed that treasure in the hand of His little child that He may use it when He needs it, but it remains always God's own treasure. Finally, it means that we must not be discouraged by our faults, for children fall frequently."[5] Thérèse's image of God as a forgiving, loving, and generous father ignited the fires of godly enthusiasm in her short life; she died at age twenty-four.

Upbringing, Education, and Experience

How we think about God does not come out of nowhere. It is often handed to us by our childhood upbringing, education, and religious formation. A friend of mine, Peter, who is in his early forties, still remembers hearing his mother's childhood threat, "Wait until your father comes home"—and that now raises his blood pressure as he prepares for the Sacrament of Reconciliation. I think I first experienced dread as I hid under the bedcovers the night after stealing a candy bar from a neighbor's kitchen; while a thunderstorm pounded the sky, all I could hear was the priest at the previous Sunday's Mass preaching about God the Father's punishment and wrath.

Some of us cannot relate to Jesus's image of God as Father. We might find it even distasteful or distressing because of the relationship with our own fathers. Rest assured, the image of God as Father is not the key that unlocks Jesus's insight into God. The key is what the image *conveys*: the reality of God's unconditional love, total acceptance, compassionate mercy, and unrelenting protection. For Jesus, fatherhood points to God's urgent longing to be in a relationship with us. So whatever image from your upbringing, education, and experience best conveys that reality—be it friend, lover, spouse, shepherd, father, or mother—is the perfect image for you to settle upon. The importance of a healthy image of God lies not in the metaphorical shape it takes but in the godly enthusiasm it sparks, enkindles, and fuels for a life of loving service.

Changing and Evolving

We develop a healthy image of God over time. The first image of God that I can remember goes back to the beginning of my teens: God was an all-knowing, all-powerful judge who had a stern but fair sense of justice. In my later teens and early twenties, the image evolved into a compassionate, merciful father who identified with my disappointments and struggles; in hindsight, this image probably emerged because of my father's suicide and the subsequent loss of a father's presence in my early adulthood. During my years of missionary activity in mainland China as I struggled with the isolation that foreigners often feel, God was an ever-present companion who loved me unconditionally and offered a tender shoulder of compassion when I needed it. Now as I approach seventy years of age, I think of God as the loving and enthusiastic conductor of the symphony of my life who, much to my utter surprise, calls out of me a melody I never knew existed.

Don't worry when you find your image of God changing over the years. That's natural as we grow and mature. An image of God that has remained static for decades can suggest that we have stopped growing spiritually or that we have come to idolize a mere picture—because, in the end, that's all an image of God is, a picture, not the person. If we are pliable, the Spirit will transform our image of God as the Spirit transforms us into the image of Christ.

Inadequacy of an Image

As I followed Hurricane Katrina and watched it destroy my hometown of New Orleans in August 2005, I couldn't help asking, how could God possibly permit this to happen? That very question is a subtle reminder that every image of God is incomplete, inferior, and inadequate. Like the seven blind men who each touched a different part of the elephant's body and then thought their description of the elephant was accurate, so too we think our images precisely and faithfully describe the reality of God. But they don't.

Some Scripture scholars suggest that this was the sin of the early Israelites in the desert (see Exodus 32:1–6). In their desire for a comprehensive image of the Lord, they took their rings and earrings and fashioned a golden calf, proclaimed it as their liberating God, and worshiped it—"These are your gods, O Israel, who brought you up out of the land of Egypt!" (Exodus 32:4). This is idolatry. The literal translations of the Hebrew words translated elsewhere as *idols* say it in a blunt way: "powerless ones," "pellets of dung," "shameful things." God cannot be contained by anything composed of human hands or the human mind.

Though there is always a temptation to fall in love with our image of God, it's important to remember that God is utter and profound mystery: incomprehensible, ineffable, unexplainable, indescribable, and unfathomable. I can't state this point any more succinctly than did St. Augustine: "If you understand it, it is not God."[6]

Not only are language, concepts, and images straitjackets when it comes to describing God, but also they can be deceptive. Yet without them, God becomes like a nebulous and amorphous cloud that doesn't spark godly enthusiasm—much less a desire to grow in the image of Christ. We need images of God more for the inspiration they incite and ignite in our lives than for the information, inadequate as it is, that they impart.

> Be perfect, therefore, as your heavenly Father is perfect.
>
> Matthew 5:48

Reading the New Testament, especially the Gospels, helps us to know, fall in love with, and imitate a God who:

- values us more than the birds and the lilies (Luke 12:22–31);
- is like a shepherd in search of one lost sheep (Luke 15:3–7);
- is like a vine-grower who prunes fruit-bearing branches to produce even more fruit (John 15:1–2);
- is a thrilled father who barrels down a dusty path to welcome a wayward son (Luke 15:11–32);
- is a gracious and generous heavenly father who makes the sun shine on the evil and the good and sends rain on the righteous and on the unrighteous (Matthew 5:45);
- is a diligent woman meticulously looking for a lost coin (Luke 15:8– 10);
- is a divine almsgiver who provides true bread from heaven (John 6:32–33);
- is like a party-thrower who invites the marginalized to a sumptuous banquet (Luke 14:15–24);
- is like a compassionate king who forgives a slave's large debt (Matthew 18:23–35).

A healthy image of God, rooted in the teachings and ministry of Jesus, fuels our enthusiasm, openness, and trust in the transformation that the Spirit eagerly wants to initiate within us.

■ REFLECT

1. What was your earliest image of God? How has that image changed over time?

2. What is your current, most common, image of God? How does it foster or challenge you to loving service of your neighbor? How does it hinder you?

3. Have you ever experienced God as an unexplainable, ineffable mystery? What was your response to this experience?

CHAPTER 8

PRINCIPLES OF PRAYER

∎

My grandmother was a pious widow in New Orleans. I still have memories of how every afternoon at 3:30, she would turn off the television and spend the next ninety minutes, as she put it, "saying my prayers." She would read most of them out of prayer books stacked on the small end table next to her lounge chair. She also kept a list of intentions for which she would pray.

I distinctly remember the day she confessed to me "the prayer of last resort." "Albert," she confided, "when Jesus turns a deaf ear to me, I never get upset. I simply take my statue of the Blessed Mother, wrap it in aluminum foil, put it in the freezer, and say, 'Jesus, your Mama is in the deep freeze, and she's not coming out until you answer my prayer!' And you know what?" she continued with a twinkle in her eye, "It usually works."

A Definition of Prayer

Gram's way of praying was unique, and yes, a bit eccentric. I am not recommending that we all pray like my dear grandmother. However, anyone serious about keeping their fire for God kindled must pray.

Prayer is one of the three CPR essentials (community, prayer, and repentance) that we intentionally adopt as we respond to God's awakening grace; it provides kindling for the spark from God. Over the course of my life, I've learned that my grandmother, at least as I perceive it, saw part of the prayer picture. But there is so much more to this practice than reading what others have prayed, saying prayers learned by rote, or twisting God's arm to respond to a request. Teresa of Avila, the sixteenth-century Carmelite reformer, mystic, and doctor of the Church, offers us the most fundamental definition of prayer when she refers to prayer as an intimate friendship, a frequent heart-to-heart conversation with him by whom we know ourselves to be loved.[7] Some important principles arise from this definition.

- *Prayer should make us prayerful.* Whatever we do when we pray—whether it's saying a rosary, reading the prayers of the saints, spending time in reflective silence, meditating on a Scripture passage, or expressing our worries and concerns to God—should make us more aware of the presence of God, who constantly surrounds us and never leaves us. People who pray typically experience God's presence while ironing, commuting to work, and walking to the dorm more often than people who don't.

There is a subtle temptation to think of my daily prayer time as just another item on my "to do" list and once I've "gotten it in," I can go about the business of the day. Such an understanding confines my awareness of God's presence to the time I spend in intentional prayer. It doesn't fuel my awareness of God's presence *during* the day nor does it fuel my loving response to the unmet need or required duty of the present moment.

Joe is the lead pastor in a large Baptist church in Texas. He has found a manageable way not only to avoid confining his prayer time to minutes on a clock but also to expand its effects throughout his day. Five times a day—before breakfast, at mid-morning, before lunch, at mid-afternoon, and before dinner—he deliberately pauses for ten minutes. He sits down, closes his eyes, and simply calls to mind the presence of God that surrounds him like the air he breathes. Once his cell phone announces the ten minutes are up, he continues with the business of the day. "This method keeps the presence of God front and center in my awareness and sustains my sensitivity to God's presence in the ordinary tasks of the day," he confided to me. Joe's prayer is keeping him prayerful.

- *We each have our own way to pray.* If prayer is supposed to make us sensitive to the God by whom we know ourselves to be loved, the God who has a burning desire to be in a relationship with us, then we will each have our own way to grow in that sensitivity. There is no one-size-fits-all method of prayer. One challenge during the way of purgation as we begin the spiritual journey is to become comfortable with our own intimate way of conversing with God. This is easier said than done. It usually takes time and some trial and error to find the method that works for each one of us personally.

- *We pray from where we are and not from where we think we should be.* Some people believe they should be further along in their prayer life, that they shouldn't get bogged down with concerns or worries about their practical, nitty-gritty lives. Consequently, they ignore their feelings and often pray around them—they pray "from the neck up," as someone once told me. Others might try to work themselves up into an emotional high or manufacture an inner space of peace, attempting to be someone they are not. In all three instances, prayer devolves into playacting as people put on their shoes, turn up the music, and tap dance for Jesus.

Such approaches ignore the fundamental fact about prayer: it is a heart-to-heart conversation. This means we should pray *from* our feelings—"from the neck down"—and not *around* them.

Alice has the right idea about prayer. "I call it my 'Come as You Are' prayer," she told me. "If I am angry, I verbalize my anger. If I am depressed, I pray from my sadness. If I am happy, I pray with joyful words of gratitude. If I am lonely, I let God know my grief."

As in any conversation with an intimate lover, we are challenged to be authentic and transparent with God. This is partly the reason why the tax collector went home "justified" after his prayer in the temple (see Luke 18:9–14). He prayed from the awareness of his sinfulness.

- *The prayers of petition and intercession are expressions of care, concern, and compassion; they are not ways to convince or coax a change of God's will.* Petition and intercession are often thought of as rain dances or ways to strong-arm God. "If I pray long enough and in the right way, I'll get what I want" is a typical attitude similar to my grandmother's.

But prayers of petition and intercession are really ways to express the first element of CPR: community, our love and interest in the lives of others. They also show our trust in God's fiery passion to be in a relationship with us and in God's loving concern for us.

- *Frustration in prayer is a sign we are trying too hard.* Frustration is a good indicator that we are not really praying from where we are, that perhaps we are trying to manufacture a spiritual feeling or arrive at a spiritual location where we currently aren't. In both cases, we are being less than honest in our conversation with God. It might also be a sign that we are actively resisting the transformative process initiated by the Spirit of God. We are trying too hard—running away from our true feelings, pushing ourselves to a place where we haven't arrived, or resisting God's grace.

As master of novices, the famed Trappist Thomas Merton was responsible for teaching young monks the fundamentals of the spiritual journey. One day, suspecting that a novice was trying too hard to pray, Merton advised him, "Brother, how does an apple ripen? It just sits in the sun."[8]

That's great advice for all of us when it comes to a heart-to-heart conversation with God. Prayer should free us up and unburden us; it shouldn't cause us to fidget or form beads of sweat on our brow. We come into the presence of God just as we are and allow this encounter to transform us—to "ripen" us just as the sun turns an apple from green to red.

Challenges in Prayer

- *Growth in prayer is moving from words to silence.* As in any other intimate friendship, the more time we spend in conversation with God, the less we have to say. We begin to spend more time listening. And listening often gives way to just being in the presence of the God by whom we know ourselves to be loved.

St. John Vianney used to watch a peasant enter the local church to pray. Wondering what the peasant said to God, Vianney asked. The peasant's reply was simple: "I look at him, and he just looks at me."

Maturing prayer is about loving glances. It becomes more and more simple and silent. This is not a cold, empty silence but the ecstatic silence of lovers—filled with a history of infidelities, broken promises, forgiveness, unconditional love, and an enthusiastic desire to deepen the relationship.

Beginners on the spiritual journey typically lean on *kataphatic* prayer. Kataphatic prayer uses the gifts of creation—words, meditative thoughts, songs, incense, candles, sunrises and sunsets, beautiful scenery—and makes of them a ladder to come into the presence of God. This is extraordinarily satisfying and brings feelings of peace and joy. I liken them to the feelings that gradually emerge in the early stages of a courtship.

Sooner or later, though, the ladder becomes rickety, the rungs give way, and we are no longer able to climb into the presence of God with our rosary, our meditative thoughts on Scripture, the smell of the incense, or the beauty of a simple candle flame. That's when we begin to move into *apophatic* prayer. Apophatic prayer tends to be silent and simple. It does not need the gifts of creation to come into the divine presence—for people who have moved into apophatic prayer, less is more. A single word, a quick glance at an icon, even a blank wall can lead them into the divine presence. Think of a spouse married for twenty years whose single glance across the room says it all.

It's important to know that this is a normal and natural development in the life of prayer. Peter posed the question that many spiritual directors hear in spiritual direction sessions, "My old way of praying isn't working any longer. What am I doing wrong?" Peter isn't doing anything wrong. The smells and bells of kataphatic prayer typically give way sooner or later to the simplicity of apophatic prayer. That's growth in prayer as it moves from words to silence.

If we don't know how or what to pray, it doesn't matter. [God's Spirit] does our praying in and for us, making prayer out of our wordless sighs, our aching groans.

Romans 8:26, MSG

The mistake that many of us make is we cling too tightly to our kataphatic prayer methods. We fear letting go of what is familiar and has worked in the past. When we hold these techniques tightly, we end up dousing the embers that can flame into mature prayer.

Whenever you are moved to silence, follow it, and simply sit with it. When you find yourself distracted, return to your prayer technique until the silence entices you again. And when it does, follow it again until you find yourself again distracted. The slow movement from words to silence and back to words is a sign of maturing prayer.

- *Dryness in prayer is a sign that something is happening.* There is a common misconception that if prayer becomes dry, boring, dissatisfying, or meaningless, we are doing something wrong. Nothing could be further from the truth. Dryness is always an indication that our kataphatic prayer techniques are flaming out as God takes over and teaches us new ways to communicate.

When we are not getting anything out of prayer, it's important that we continue to remain faithful to it. Just showing up every day and going through the motions is a bold act of fidelity that is blessed by God.

- *The goal of prayer is not a mind free of distractions but a surrendered heart of love.* Every time I pray, I have distractions. My mind seems stoked with green wood that crackles, hisses, pops, and shoots sparks everywhere. My attention follows those sparks and I become discouraged as I struggle to rid myself of the distractions; to make matters worse, the very effort to rid myself of them becomes another distraction!

Two things are worth mentioning. First, distractions are not as bad as you might think. They are certainly not sins that need to be confessed. As a matter of fact, they can be great teachers in the spiritual life. They sometimes indicate our passions and investments in life. They might also point out areas where our weaknesses and sins throw water on the kindling. In both cases, distractions can tell us exactly where we are and become the topics for our heart-to-heart conversation with the God by whom we know ourselves to be loved.

Second, the aim of prayer is not the attainment of some Zen-like, thoughtless state of consciousness. Its fundamental aim is a heart-to-heart conversation in which we learn openness to the call and challenge of the Spirit to lovingly respond to the unmet need or required duty of the present moment. As we grow in prayer and are transformed into the image of Christ, we pray the psalm that the letter to the Hebrews places on the lips of Christ, "See, God, I have come to do your will, O God" (Hebrews 10:7; Psalm 40:7–8).

My grandmother's practice of putting a statue in the freezer as a prayer of last resort was unquestionably strange, certainly superstitious, and maybe downright manipulative. But it also bespeaks an intimate friendship, a godly enthusiasm, and a good-natured humor that are at the root of any heart-to-heart conversation with a beloved.

■ REFLECT

1. In what ways does your current method of prayer match Teresa of Avila's description of prayer? In what ways does it not?
2. How do you deal with feelings and distractions in prayer? When have they become your teachers in the spiritual life?
3. When was the last time you felt frustrated or dry in prayer? Upon reflection, what was the cause? How did you handle the frustration or dryness?

CHAPTER 9

THE ATTITUDE OF GRATITUDE

∎

Prayer is not the only time-tested kindling for the fire of godly enthusiasm. There is also the attitude of gratitude, and it builds upon both a healthy image of God and a vibrant, intentional prayer life.

As David Steindl-Rast, OSB, so wisely states on his popular website, www.gratefulness.org, "In daily life we must see that it is not happiness that makes us grateful, but gratefulness that makes us happy." Gratitude transforms us into children who recognize their dependence and who realize that everything is a grace, gift, and blessing from a good God. In God's generous bidding to have a relationship with us, God spreads before us an exquisite table called the banquet of life and offers us everything we need. God enthusiastically invites, "Come to the feast!" As invited guests to this banquet, we can never point to anything and say, "This is mine"—except for our sins. Everything else comes from the generosity of God.

G. K. Chesterton, the English writer and Christian apologist, wrote, "You say grace before meals. All right. But I say grace before the concert and the opera, and grace before the play and pantomime, and grace before I open a book, and grace before sketching, painting, swimming, fencing, boxing, walking, playing, dancing and grace before I dip the pen in the ink."[9] God's grace is the unquestionable foundation of life, and gratitude is the first response.

That realization gave a unique twist to the poverty of Francis of Assisi. Unlike the monastic understanding of his time, which interpreted poverty as a form of self-denial, Francis's poverty was born of a radical affirmation that God can be trusted to provide for everything—from a helping hand in times of loneliness to food, clothing, and shelter.

Toward the end of his life, Francis reflected upon his forty-four years and wrote unabashedly in his *Testament* how God was always ready to provide for his needs. No less than four times he uses the expression, "The Lord gave me . . ." All was gift and grace: the beginning of his conversion and ministry to the lepers, his faith, his respect for priests, and the brothers who joined him. Awareness of God's providence not only fueled Francis's understanding of poverty and his attitude of gratitude, but it is also a stunning reminder to us that worry and anxiety are insults to God.

Obstacles to a Grateful Heart

The crippling effects of worry and anxiety are not the only obstacles to gratitude. I note two others. The first is that many of us are so busy multitasking that we never stop long enough to reflect and become aware of the many people, events, and situations the Spirit uses to touch us and transform our lives. I tend to do this myself.

At least twice a month, I pack a bag, schedule an Uber ride, and head to the airport to catch a flight. That forty-minute ride would provide an excellent time to sit back and reflect upon my life. But instead of thinking and praying about how God is speaking to me in these airport trips and my ministry, I usually spend the time checking my e-mails, revising my presentations, and replying to voicemail messages. Socrates might have been speaking directly to me when he said, "The unexamined life is not worth living"! Constant multitasking hinders me from fanning the embers that can flare up into the flame of gratitude.

The second additional obstacle to gratitude comes when we forget how God's grace and goodness helped us through past tragedies and major disappointments. We fail to recognize and remember how

God cares for us in our small, daily routines. To ignore or forget God's goodness to us, or to give credit to anyone else, is to be found guilty of arson.

Growing in Gratitude

Since I have struggled in the past to give gratitude the attention it deserves, let me tell you what I have learned. There are practices that are helpful in fostering a spirit of gratefulness and appreciation, that make our lives worry-free and happier.

The eighteenth-century French clergyman and revolutionary Jean-Baptiste Massieu famously said, *La reconnaissance est la mémoire du cœur* ("Gratitude is the memory of the heart"). *Reconnaissance* has the sense of recognizing or literally "reknowing." That recognition, "reknowing," and gratitude are forged with *daily reflection and mindful awareness*. One of my spiritual directees spends ten minutes a day reflecting upon her life and remembering the many ways God has blessed her. Sometimes she surveys the broad strokes of her fifty years of life; other times she sits in gratitude and praise for a surprise visit from a friend, a sunny day, or a freshly brewed cup of coffee. She continually tells me that daily reflection and mindful awareness help to expand her heart as she comes to see the utter gratuity of the marvelous and the mundane.

The Jewish theologian Abraham Joshua Heschel once walked into his New York classroom and announced, "An incredible thing happened as I was walking over here to class." This comment piqued the curiosity of his students, who asked what he'd seen. Heschel responded, "The sun set. The sun set and no one on Broadway noticed it."[10]

Heschel reminds us of the importance of *wonder and awe*. When we take the time to reflect not only on our life's journey but also on life itself, we get a sense of the magic in the air. And that drives us to our knees in thanks. The fingernails of a newborn baby, a shooting star streaking across the sky, the oddity of a Venus fly trap, the howling of a coyote, and the beauty of the Alps pull us out of ourselves and reveal something bigger than ourselves. And that "something" is a Creator who is enthusiastic about being in a relationship with us.

When I look at your heavens, the work of your fingers, the moon and the stars that you have established; what are human beings that you are mindful of them, mortals that you care for them?

Psalm 8:3-4

The magnificent creativity of God and our awe at the lavishness of life lead us to an awareness of who we really are. Knowing that we are invited guests to the banquet of life fuels the virtue of *humility* that grounds all gratitude. Derived from the Latin word *humus*, meaning dirt or ground, humility keeps our feet on the ground as it raises up our eyes to God in thanks and praise. There is no authentic gratitude without the awareness of our unworthiness and insignificance.

Living in a world of progress reports, report cards, and performance evaluations, we are often tempted to take ourselves too seriously. What would it feel like to rediscover a childlike sense of *joy and playfulness* that connects you to the inherent goodness of life? A game of pitch-and-catch with an eight-year-old son? Playing house with a niece? Making up a bedtime story, walking the dog, finding a coworker to play Rock-Paper-Scissors, going for a swim, or dressing up with hat and boots and square dancing with a spouse? These activities can be spiritual practices that open us to a dimension of life that we, as adults, don't often experience. Far from a cynical question, "Are we having fun yet?" is an excellent reminder of the importance of joy and laughter. The mystic and saint Teresa of Avila rightly reminded her community that a sad nun is a bad nun. We grow old and ungrateful when we stop playing, teasing, and laughing.

Gratitude and appreciation form the warp and weft of every invited guest's clothing. They are so basic and essential for our spiritual transformation that Meister Eckhart, a fourteenth-century Dominican mystic, said, *Haete der mensche niht me ze tuonne mit gote, dan daz er dankbaere ist, ez waere genuoc* ("If a man had no more to do with God than to be thankful, that would suffice").[11]

■ REFLECT

1. How has a spirit of gratitude shaped your lifestyle and spiritual practice? When are you more prone to gratitude? To ingratitude?
2. Where does pride still reign in your life? Why?
3. When and how was the last time you played and laughed? Did it help foster a spirit of gratitude and appreciation for life? How can playfulness and joy be better incorporated into your spiritual journey?

CHAPTER 10

THE DIVINE MILIEU

■

I once asked several people who come to me for spiritual direction where they find God. I was surprised to get many different answers. Belinda said, "I see God in the second-grade children I teach. Their innocence, joy, and wonder often remind me that God is closer than I have ever thought or imagined." Mike, a Protestant minister, replied, "I find God in Scripture. In his Word, God reveals to me his divine love and forgiveness. In my opinion, that's all we need in life." Sister Catherine, a pastoral associate in a large suburban Catholic parish, said, "I find God within. Years ago I read a mystic who talked about the 'sanctuary of the soul,' and so every day I spend time in prayer, going within to encounter my God." Bill, who is legally blind, replied, "I see God in the gift of the Eucharist."

The Divine Milieu

As I listened to these replies, I couldn't help remembering Augustine's definition of a sacrament: "a visible sign of an invisible reality."[12] My directees' different answers and Augustine's definition make me aware that, in a broad sense, our existence is sacramental: many earthly realities reveal God's existence, God's merciful compassion, and God's urgent longing to be in a relationship with us. We live in a "divine milieu," to borrow a phrase from the Jesuit philosopher and paleontologist Pierre Teilhard de Chardin.

Two thousand years ago, God walked this earth in the person of Jesus called Emmanuel, "God is with us" (Matthew 1:23), love made flesh. "Whoever has seen me has seen the Father" (John 14:9). Jesus is not only the full manifestation of God on the spiritual journey but

also is himself the path. "I am the way
. . . No one comes to the Father except
through me" (John 14:6).

As twenty-first-century believers,
we are not at a disadvantage in meeting
Jesus. We too can encounter him in
another way that boggles my mind and
that I don't always appreciate: in the
poor, the marginalized, and those who
have no voice in society. "Truly I tell
you, just as you did it to one of the least
of these who are members of my family,

> He is the image of
> the invisible God,
> the firstborn of
> all creation. . . .
> For in him all the fullness
> of God was pleased to
> dwell.
>
> Colossians 1:15, 19

you did it to me" (Matthew 25:40); "Whoever welcomes this child in
my name welcomes me, and whoever welcomes me welcomes the one
who sent me" (Luke 9:48). Those who have no personal resources to
fall back upon and who live with outstretched hands reveal the humility
of God who was born in a stable and died on a cross.

The gathered Christian community—the church—also continues the presence of Jesus in our midst: "For where two or three are
gathered in my name, I am there among them" (Matthew 18:20). The
love shown to our neighbors and that we are blessed to receive from
others, the forgiveness both offered and obtained, and the merciful
compassion that wells up in the hearts of believers, all are fragmentary
expressions of God's unfathomable love, forgiveness, and compassion
revealed in Jesus.

Furthermore, as embodied spirits with the gifts of self-awareness,
reflection, and creativity, we mirror in our limited, human way the
image of God (Genesis 1:27). We are also temples of God's indwelling
Spirit (1 Corinthians 3:16), who seeks to transform us ever more into
the image of Christ. In a word, we ourselves are visible signs of an
invisible reality.

Sacraments and Scripture

We also encounter the continuing ministry of Christ in the sacraments of the Church. There, Jesus is fully alive! The Catechism of the Catholic Church defines sacraments as "efficacious signs of grace, instituted by Christ and entrusted to the Church, by which divine life is dispensed to us" (#1131). These actions of the Church make present ("efficacious signs") an encounter with God ("grace"). They are heavenly treasures on earth. Each of them is rooted in the life and ministry of Jesus: his baptism in the Jordan (baptism); his forgiveness of sins (reconciliation); his gift of the Holy Spirit to aid us in our mission (confirmation); his healing ministry (anointing of the sick); his first miracle at Cana recorded in the Gospel of John (matrimony); his choice of Peter and the apostles (sacerdotal and episcopal ordination); his table ministry and last supper before his death (Eucharist). Though Christian denominations disagree on the exact number of the sacraments instituted by Christ, they do agree that using ordinary things such as water, oil, a gesture, bread and wine, under certain conditions, provides sparks for the fire of godly enthusiasm in our lives.

And then we encounter the divine in the Scriptures. In the written word of God, the Father of creation tells us about his burning desire to be in a relationship with us; that is what salvation history is all about. In the pages of Scripture we come face-to-face with our vocation to be transformed into the image of Christ, sent to lovingly respond to the unmet need and required duty of the present moment. Unlike contemporary novels and short stories, Scripture is "living and active, sharper than any two-edged sword" (Hebrews 4:12), used by the Spirit as a tool in the process of our transformation.

The Books of Creation and Life

If sacraments are visible signs of invisible realities, then creation too is sacramental; its qualities and design betray the creativity and wisdom of its author. Some medieval theologians even referred to it as the first book written by God. Though there is a clear distinction between the Creator and creation, all created things, from trees and turnips, armadillos and aardvarks, to hippopotamuses and humans, bear the signature of the Creator and give us a glimpse of God; indeed, every page of this book has been handwritten by the divine. No wonder the Franciscan mystic Angela of Foligno said that the world is "pregnant with God."[13]

Celtic spirituality offers beautiful reflections and interpretations of how this works. These ancient Christian teachings propose that some places are especially *thin*, meaning that here the supposed wall separating the divine from the human is exceptionally low and permeable. Perhaps you have felt this at some time in your own life. I experienced this in an extraordinary way when I walked the grounds of Dachau concentration camp and felt the grief of God. I again felt God's majesty as I flew over the vast Sahara desert, and then later God's abiding presence while praying in Chartres cathedral. I've also experienced the divine presence in the silence of a local forest preserve and at the graves of my parents in New Orleans. Whether natural landscapes or holy places of pilgrimage made by human hands, these locations and others are the meeting grounds for God and the human race; in these places we palpably experience the closeness of the divine.

All of these—the person of Jesus, a neighbor in need or in the church, our physical bodies, the Church's sacraments, Scripture, creation, and thin places—glimmer and glow with the presence of God, reminding us that we live in a divine milieu. This awareness is further kindling that has the potential to set us ablaze.

■ REFLECT

1. Where do you typically "find" God? How do you respond to the divine presence in your life?

2. Of the visible realities pointing to God mentioned in this chapter—Jesus, a neighbor in need or in the church, our physical bodies, the sacraments, Scripture, creation, and thin places—which one do you find the most challenging? The most comforting?

3. When was the last time you felt the closeness of God? Where were you? What feelings did it elicit from you?

CHAPTER 11

ME, MYSELF, AND I: True or False?

∎

During a spiritual direction session, a directee once said to me, "I so easily identify with Saint Paul when he says, 'I do not understand my own actions. For I do not do what I want, but I do the very thing I hate'" (Romans 7:15).

When I asked her to explain, she said, "I love to buy handbags. And I know it! I also know that I have too many handbags for anyone to use. So I really try and stop myself from buying more of them. But then, all of a sudden, if I am a little bit sad or if I need a little emotional lift—after all, we're supposed to be happy, right?—I see this stranger sit in front of the computer, go to a website like Amazon, and buy another handbag. And that stranger, believe it or not, is *me*! I just don't understand. I know the thrill of buying another handbag isn't going to last forever, but I keep thinking it will, and so I keep doing it."

I thought it most interesting and right on target that she referred to "this stranger." In her own way, she was experiencing what we call the "false self."

The Energy Centers of the False Self

There is a demanding, irrational, and sometimes spoiled stranger inside each one of us. And this stranger often tries to throw water on our kindling by convincing us to do things we know better not to do or often don't want to do.

Taking an expression made popular by Thomas Merton in his writings from the 1960s, another Trappist monk, the late Thomas Keating, OCSO, called this stranger inside us the "false self." This false self is obsessed with self-concern, self-interest, self-gratification, and self-preservation. It equates happiness with satisfying the instinctual needs of these ego-obsessions by running after power and control, survival and security, a need for affection, the desire for esteem and pleasure, and cultural or group identification. Keating sometimes refers to these needs as the "emotional energy centers."

Some adults become obsessed with power and control, seeking endless ways to amass prestige, dominate others, and impose their wills. Some are never satisfied with their bank accounts or possessions, greedily chasing after big money, gadgets, and stuff. Still others go on a quixotic search for love and self-esteem, looking in all the wrong places, whether it be dimly lit street corners or the approving smiles of anyone or everyone. And still others find strength in numbers, joining organizations and groups of people with varying agendas—just as long as they give a sense of approval, acceptance, and most of all, inclusion.

These energy centers get solidified early in life, and somewhere along the line, as we live without self-reflection, we become convinced that we *need* to satisfy one or more of them *in order to be happy*. Yes, we all need some power, security, and love to have healthy adult self-images. But the false self takes that to the extreme and persuades us of its deceptive agenda: happiness comes *solely* from the emotional lift provided by buying a handbag, joining groups or being with other people, or feeling love. As soon as that emotional energy center has been momentarily satisfied, the thrill dissipates, and we see that we have once again been double-crossed and conned. The more we feed the obsessions with self-concern, self-interest, self-gratification, and self-preservation, the more they expand in our lives and continue to control us.

I've discovered that the false self isn't just invested in acquiring "empty P's" like power, possessions, prestige, pleasure, and popularity. It's also insistent on avoiding pain, blame, criticism, disgrace, and loss. Criticize me or try and inflict emotional pain on me—and you'll instantly hear me justifying, denying, rationalizing, and shaming. In many respects, the false self is the ventriloquist of the inner monologue and, when threatened, will not hesitate to move its lips to verbally defend itself.

The obsession to satisfy the desires of the energy centers and to avoid any kind of pain and criticism keeps the false self alive. That stranger continues to influence and dominate our lives as long as we indulge its agenda.

Jesus and the True Self

Jesus directly confronted the false self's agenda to acquire comforts and avoid pain. On several occasions, he taught a new way of living, freed from the stranglehold of the false self:

- "Do not fear those who kill the body but cannot kill the soul; rather fear him who can destroy both soul and body in hell" (Matthew 10:28).

- "Therefore I tell you, do not worry about your life, what you will eat or what you will drink, or about your body, what you will wear. Is not life more than food, and the body more than clothing?" (Matthew 6:25).

- "If any want to become my followers, let them deny themselves and take up their cross daily and follow me" (Luke 9:23).

Do not resist the evil-doer. But if anyone strikes you on the right cheek, turn the other also; and if anyone wants to sue you and take your coat, give your cloak as well; and if anyone forces you to go one mile, go also the second mile.

Matthew 5:39–41

- "Love your enemies and pray for those who persecute you" (Matthew 5:44).

The Spirit acts upon this wisdom of Jesus as the Spirit disengages us from the self-serving agenda of the false self and transforms us into the image of Christ sent to live with radical trust in God and uncompromising love of neighbor. This is the "true self," the person God intends for us to be, and is characterized by the fruit of the Spirit: "love, joy, peace, patience, kindness, generosity, faithfulness, gentleness, and self-control" (Galatians 5:22–23).

Yet the false self protests this transformation, pushes back, and resists. And that resistance is based upon fear. The false self is terrified of a life without the emotional highs of power, possessions, prestige, pleasure, and popularity; it dreads a life of pain and disgrace.

That resistance gets translated into emotional frustration as we struggle to satisfy the energy centers and defend ourselves against any kind of criticism or loss. Ever wonder why you feel so frustrated? Much of it is self-imposed as you doggedly cling to the false self's egocentric agenda and refuse the transformation offered by the Spirit.

The Beatitudes of Jesus as presented in Matthew (5:3–11) offer us a way to break free of the self-imposed frustration caused by our preoccupation with the ego-obsessions. They also help us prepare kindling for the spark of the Spirit:

- Attacking the selfish agenda of the false self head-on, Jesus tells those of us who are obsessed with possessions and pride, "Blessed are the poor in spirit, for theirs is the kingdom of heaven" (verse 3).
- Those of us on the hunt for emotional highs and pleasure are reminded, "Blessed are those who mourn, for they will be comforted" (verse 4).

- An obsession with power will not give us what we think it will: "Blessed are the meek, for they will inherit the earth" (verse 5).

- We miss the mark when we try and dodge the criticism and disgrace that comes with standing up for the truth: "Blessed are those who hunger and thirst for righteousness, for they will be filled" (verse 6).

- A duplicitous life of serving the agenda of the false self while trying to catch fire clouds one's vision: "Blessed are the pure in heart, for they will see God" (verse 8).

- Those who are aggressive and defensive and seek revenge are warned, "Blessed are the merciful, for they will receive mercy," and "Blessed are the peacemakers, for they will be called children of God" (verses 7, 9).

- And there is an ultimate and lasting payoff for those who submit to pain, blame, criticism, and disgrace: "Blessed are you when people revile you and persecute you and utter all kinds of evil against you falsely on my account. Rejoice and be glad, for your reward is great in heaven, for in the same way they persecuted the prophets who were before you" (verses 11–12).

It's important to recall that our transformation into the image of Christ is a lifelong process. Consequently, we never die completely to the false self and live fully from the reality of the true self. But we do get glimpses of the true self in moments when we live the Beatitudes, love selflessly, forgive unconditionally, rediscover the fleeting nature of power and possessions, and experience the transformative nature of suffering.

With a succinct pointedness, Jesus clearly demonstrates that there is a new kind of logic at work as the Spirit begins the process of our transformation. By living the Beatitudes and using Jesus's wisdom as kindling, we facilitate the Spirit's action of setting our lives on fire.

■ REFLECT

1. What do you think you *need* in order to be happy? How is this belief a source of anxiety and frustration in your life?

2. What methods and techniques do you use to avoid pain, blame, criticism, disgrace, and loss? Why do you refuse to accept these things?

3. How do the Beatitudes of Jesus challenge your current thoughts and actions? Which of them speaks the most to you?

CHAPTER 12

GOD AND SUFFERING

■

Widowed at the age of forty-two by my father's suicide, my mother had only a high school diploma, no professional skills, a debt of $60,000, and three of her five children left at home still to raise. By God's grace coupled with her sacrificial spirit and innate tenacity, she would attend the college graduation of her three boys and retire as a computer administrator for a national insurance company. All five of her children had hoped her retirement would be filled with the joys of being a grandmother and the pride of having two daughters in the convent and one son an ordained priest.

But her retirement didn't turn out that way. It was marred by confusion and erratic mood swings. Alzheimer's disease began to blanket this once feisty, vivacious woman and reduce her to smoldering ashes.

As I watched her life flame out, I often asked, why did God allow someone who had suffered so much to come to such an undignified end? Why did God allow my mother to suffer for so many years with the gnawing guilt of a spouse's suicide? Why hadn't God intervened and performed a miracle to ease her emotional suffering and physical hardships?

My mother had chosen to be cremated. When the funeral director handed me the small square urn that contained her ashes, I wondered, why doesn't God improve his reputation and respond to requests to alleviate suffering in the world? It would certainly entice and excite others to follow the Spirit more intentionally.

Scripture and Suffering

We all have had the experience of praying to God and asking why. Why do children suffer? Why doesn't God stop wars? Why doesn't God intervene and stop us from enduring misery, misfortune, and malady?

These questions, left unanswered by God, have been asked since the beginning of time and often are used by some people to justify a cold disinterest in personal spiritual transformation. "Why should I be interested in the spiritual life when God seems so cold and cruel?" a friend once remarked.

Further, the different rationales and diverse reasons that some people have given for suffering don't always sit well with us even though they can be justified with reference to the Scriptures. Some of the typical scriptural reasons include these:

- *God uses suffering as punishment for sin.* The Old Testament begins with God punishing the original parents' disobedience with the pangs of childbirth and the toil of labor (see Genesis 3:16–19). The books of Judges, Samuel, Kings, and many of the prophets amplify this idea by portraying God as a judge who blesses the chosen people with prosperity and success when they are faithful but quickly punishes when they turn away and begin to worship idols. According to this interpretation, God's severest punishment came with the chosen people's exile from the promised land: "And the nations shall know that the house of Israel went into captivity for their iniquity, because they dealt treacherously with me [says the LORD God]" (Ezekiel 39:23).

- *God is not the cause.* Jesus distances his Abba from the image of a judge who punishes those who sin. His father shows no favoritism, since he lets the sun rise on the good and the evil and sends rain on the righteous and the unrighteous (see

Matthew 5:45). He dismisses the idea that suffering or sickness is a punishment for sin (see Luke 13:1–5; John 9:3). However, he makes clear that discipleship does not insulate us from potential pain and suffering; it involves taking up our crosses and losing our lives for his and the gospel's sake (see Mark 8:34–35).

- *Suffering is good even though we cannot always see why.* Scripture sometimes highlights how God brings good out of suffering. In the Old Testament, Joseph saw how God had used his suffering for the greater good of numerous people (see Genesis 50:15–21). In the New Testament, Peter, echoing Isaiah's suffering servant (see Isaiah 53:4–5), interprets Christ's suffering as the very means of our redemption: "[Christ] himself bore our sins in his body on the cross, so that, free from sins, we might live for righteousness; by his wounds you have been healed" (1 Peter 2:24).

- *Suffering can be a form of God's discipline.* Proverbs states that suffering is the discipline and reproof of a loving God (see Proverbs 3:11–12). The letter to the Hebrews comments explicitly on this proverb and highlights the transformative powers of this kind of discipline: the Father of spirits "disciplines us for our good, in order that we may share his holiness" (Hebrews 12:10).

- *Suffering can be character building.* Though he does not mention God's role in it, Paul notes the pride we should take in suffering, since it builds up in us endurance, character, and hope (Romans 5:1–5).

- *The devil causes suffering.* The New Testament offers still another interpretation of suffering. God's enemy, the demons (Luke 9:38–39), evil spirits (Acts 19:11–12), Satan (Luke 13:16) or the devil (Acts 10:38), are sometimes depicted in ways that make it seem that they are the cause of all sickness and diseases.

Our Response

You can clearly see that there isn't one consistent scriptural answer for the question, *why suffering?* Each of these answers occasionally can be helpful, while in some circumstances—like African starvation, AIDS, Alzheimer's disease, or the death of a loved one—they might seem blatantly cruel. A few might be helpful for you but not for me. Some might make sense only in hindsight; others might seem totally senseless or downright silly.

Trying to come to terms with an adequate answer to the question of suffering is doomed to frustration and maybe even failure. The book of Job attempts to answer it and, frankly, comes up short. I've racked my brains for years and have read virtually every book on the topic and I still walk around with this question gnawing in my heart.

I'm often accused of opting out of any discussion on the question, *why suffering?* Rather than trying to answer the question *why*, which might only satisfy the intellectually curious, perhaps the more important questions to ask are: *How* do we live with the mystery of suffering? *How* do we prepare kindling for the spark from a supposedly loving God when agony or distress has blanketed our soul? Here, the biblical tradition does, in fact, offer us some helpful answers.

Face the suffering and cry out. We typically shy away from suffering. We do our best to medicate ourselves against it, often encouraging each other to keep a stiff upper lip and, "Don't worry, be happy."

Scripture, however, challenges us to face the suffering and lament. Psalms such as 3, 5, 10, 17, 22, 38, 44, 77, 88, and 109 suggest we pray "from the neck down" and cry out to God from the depths of our sadness and pain. Far from betraying disbelief or doubt in God, the prayer of lament is a profound expression of trust in God's ultimate power and vindication. That's why we shouldn't fear divine anger or retribution when praying it.

Hang on to faith in God. Lamenting allows us to stay connected to God with even the thinnest thread of faith. Psalm 22 reminds us that faith is sometimes mined in hindsight, by remembering times past when our or others' prayers were answered: "To you [our ancestors] cried, and were saved" (verse 5).

The encouragement of Scripture is that God gives heed to hope fashioned out of helplessness (Psalm 138:3; 2 Corinthians 1:8–11; Philippians 1:19–20). Anguish raised in prayer is always addressed by Providence.

Surrender. As we lament in our anguish, we must also realize that suffering is often a mystery. Though Christian responsibility and prudence challenge us to extricate ourselves from abusive situations or follow the

My God, my God, why have you forsaken me? Why are you so far from helping me, from the words of my groaning? O my God, I cry by day, but you do not answer; and by night, but find no rest. . . . In you our ancestors trusted; they trusted, and you delivered them. To you they cried, and were saved; in you they trusted, and were not put to shame.

Psalm 22:1–2, 4–5

wise advice of medical science, some forms of suffering we can only bow before—and willingly submit to. Standing before the ineffable God who controls the seeming chaos of creation (see Job 38–40), with Job we say, "I'm speechless, in awe—words fail me. I should never have opened my mouth!" (40:4, MSG). With Shadrach, Meshach, and Abednego, we walk through the fiery furnace trusting that it is a furnace of transformation as we pray their prayer: "And now with all our heart we follow you; we fear you and seek your presence. Do not put us to shame, but deal with us in your patience and in your abundant mercy. Deliver us in accordance with your marvelous works, and bring glory to your name, O Lord" (Daniel 3:41–43). Surrendering to suffering, indeed, is the ultimate act of faith and trust for someone who wants to imitate Christ: "Father, into your hands I commend my spirit" (Luke 23:46).

Far from a problem to be solved or understood, suffering will inevitably shape and mold the contours of our souls. Facing, lamenting, and surrendering to it with even the thinnest threads of faith and trust become an inspired moment that provides kindling for godly enthusiasm during the most difficult of times.

■ REFLECT

1. How can a God of unconditional love permit suffering? How satisfying is your answer?

2. Which of the scriptural understandings of suffering ring true to your own experience? Which ones do not?

3. Reflect upon a recent moment of suffering. How did you initially respond? Have you learned anything about suffering in hindsight?

Catching

Fire

METHODS OF PRAYER

*God's fiery passion sparks kindling into flame
through a rich variety of prayer methods that stoke
the awareness of God's presence in our ordinary lives.*

CHAPTER 13

THE EXAMEN

■

One day a discouraged Christian who hadn't given much attention to his relationship with God asked the fourteenth-century Dominican mystic Meister Eckhart for a suggestion about how to make up for lost time. Eckhart replied, "Be in all things a God-seeker and at all times, a God-finder, among all kinds of people and in all kinds of circumstances. And make it a life habit to copy Jesus Christ, to do the things he did and avoid the things he avoided."[14]

You might be noticing some smoldering embers inside of you. They might be glowing with the desire for transformation so you can seek and find God in all the people and circumstances you encounter. You might be wondering how to fan those embers into flame.

Or maybe you feel like that discouraged Christian who hadn't given much attention to spiritual growth. You want to cut to the chase by finding out about spiritual practices and how to catch fire.

In either case, let's start talking about deepening our response to God.

There is a vast array of spiritual practices from which to choose. Our personality plays a big role in determining which practice or technique warms us spiritually. No one is capable of simultaneously practicing all the techniques that I'll be discussing or even finding them all helpful—and, thankfully, we are not supposed to. So pick and choose. By trial and error, you'll gradually discover which ones help you yield to the Spirit's transformation.

There is no better place to start than the Examen. Being God-seekers and God-finders is the basis of this five-hundred-year-old prayer method. People nowadays refer to the Examen as the examination of consciousness. It consists of reviewing and surveying our ordinary routine and the mundane messiness of our daily lives. This intentional practice often reveals divine sparks in the people, events, meetings, and circumstances we have just experienced. That awareness can set us on fire with godly enthusiasm.

The Practice

Saint Ignatius of Loyola is credited with proposing and promoting the Examen. He taught that it should be done twice daily, at midday and again before retiring to bed. However, his flexibility also allows for a once-daily practice. For some, mornings work better than evenings. Ignatius also taught that it should not extend excessively; fifteen minutes is ample time to reap its benefits if it is done faithfully and daily.

There are five steps to the traditional practice of the Examen. Again, Ignatius allows for flexibility. After some practice, we can adapt and tweak the steps, realizing that the goal is to become increasingly aware and conscious of the divine presence in our everyday lives. Perhaps, on some days, a person would focus on just one or two of the steps; on other days, she would complete all five steps within the allotted fifteen-minute time frame. The benefits of the practice are reaped in daily fidelity to it, not simply in getting through each of the five individual steps.

The first step of the Examen is *gratitude*. We look over our present life and thank God for any gifts, graces, or blessings we have received. This step of gratitude might focus on life's big picture and the many manifestations of God's love: spouse, children, job, home, or the inner strength that seemingly came out of nowhere to help us get through a crisis or an emotional upheaval. At other times, our gratitude might be focused like a laser beam on a specific person, event, or grace that was given to us as recently as a few hours ago. We should not be too quick to move on from this step, since growth in gratitude is growth in the conscious awareness of God's generosity to us.

Sometimes my fifteen-minute practice of the Examen consists solely of this first step. Gratitude and thanksgiving sometimes race across my soul like wildfire as I become conscious of God's encouragement and support spoken through the words of a friend or relative. Or I become attuned in a conscious way to God's gift of a sunny day, a phone call from a close friend, or an insight that God allowed me to put into words. The flames of gratitude leap up and I bask in their warmth—and in their long afterglow.

Step two is the *petition to the Holy Spirit*. Since the Spirit is the flint and fuel of godly enthusiasm and the One who transforms us into the image of Christ, we ask the Holy Spirit to open our eyes, ears, and hearts as we review the events of the past few hours since our last practice of the Examen. This is also a prayer for enlightenment and insight as we seek to understand the many and varied ways the Spirit of God calls us to spiritual transformation. This petition helps to bring the Holy Spirit front and center to our consciousness. The prayer I use is simple and short: "O Holy Spirit, heal me of my blindness and open my eyes to the divine presence in the mundane messiness of the past few hours. Heal me of my deafness and open my ears to your transformative call. Heal me of my hardheartedness and soften my heart to meet the God of disguise and surprise in the people I encountered today. Amen."

The Heart of the Examen

The *review* forms the heart and soul of the Examen. We survey and probe the immediate past hours since the last time we practiced the

Examen. Event by event, hour by hour, minute by minute, we pray through the day "rummaging for God,"[15] as one writer describes it. Questions that we ask ourselves include:

- Where was God speaking to me and challenging me?
- How was the Spirit inviting me to be more Christlike?
- When and in what circumstances was God bestowing graces, gifts, and blessings upon me?
- How was the Spirit asking me to be lovingly present in the situation in which I found myself?
- How was God asking me to humbly serve the people in front of me?
- To what unmet need or required duty was the Spirit calling me to respond?

While they were talking and discussing, Jesus himself came near and went with them, but their eyes were kept from recognizing him.

. . . Then their eyes were opened, and they recognized him; and he vanished from their sight.

(Luke 24:15–16,31)

It's important to remember that this third step is God-centered, not me-centered. That's why the Examen is called an examination of consciousness and is distinct from an examination of conscience: we look for God in the Examen and do not judge ourselves, as in an examination of conscience.

An early scene from the 1939 movie *The Wizard of Oz* might prove to be a helpful analogy for this third step. The movie begins in black-and-white. After Dorothy's house falls on the Wicked Witch of the East, Dorothy emerges from her bedroom and discovers she has landed in Munchkinland. Suddenly, the movie turns to Technicolor. Glinda the Good Witch of the North appears and invites the Munchkins to show themselves by singing, "Come out, come out, wherever you are!"

In the third step of the review, we attempt to see our lives not in the black-and-white shade of its ordinariness but in the Technicolor of its extraordinariness as a meeting place for the living God. Remember how I mentioned the "thin places" of Celtic spirituality in chapter 10? Those are the places where the supposed wall separating the divine from the human is exceptionally low and permeable. Our daily life is a thin place. And so, we turn our attention to God, rummage through the events of the day, and with Glinda the Good Witch of the North we sing, "Come out, come out, wherever you are!"

The fourth step is the *dialogue of forgiveness*. We express sorrow and ask forgiveness for still living on autopilot, unaware and unconscious of God's surrounding presence in our daily routines. This step is not supposed to be a monologue in which we scold and criticize ourselves for our insensitivity or put ourselves on a guilt trip. Rather, this step is intended to be a dialogue between God and ourselves in which we encounter a merciful, loving God who is enthusiastic about being in a relationship with us. If we walk away from this fourth step feeling guilty or remorseful, we have not done it properly. We must allow enough time to hear the consoling and forgiving words of God.

The Examen concludes with the *renewal*. In this step, we look over our upcoming daily schedule as we now know it and anticipate the approaching hours or events where we need to be particularly attentive to the pending manifestation of the divine presence or call. We renew our anticipation of God's presence in order to participate in it. We ask ourselves:

- Where might the God of disguise surprise me?
- What situation might the Spirit use to mold me ever closer into the image of Christ?
- How could God possibly use this particular person or this planned meeting to spark my godly enthusiasm into flame?

In this fifth and final step, we are recommitting ourselves to switching our lives off autopilot.

For almost twenty years, I have practiced the Examen daily. I find this simple method of prayer extraordinarily helpful in transforming me into a God-seeker, a God-finder, and someone who is aware that "[God] is not far from each one of us. For 'In him we live and move and have our being'" (Acts 17:27–28). Thanks to the Examen, I am convinced that God's passion to have a relationship with me spills over into the mundane moments of my everyday routine.

■ REFLECT

1. How often in the past week do you think you were living on autopilot? What practical ways can you adopt to become a more conscious God-seeker and God-finder?

2. Spend some time right now rummaging for God over the past few hours. How difficult do you find this to be? How do you know it's really God and not just your imagination?

3. Which of the five specific steps of the Examen would help you catch the flame of godly enthusiasm most of all? Is there anything stopping you from practicing the Examen, and that step, now?

CHAPTER 14

MEDITATION AND CONTEMPLATION

■

Peter had been coming to spiritual direction for about six months. During one session he admitted, "I think I am losing ground in the spiritual life and going backward. For a few months, I had felt that God was really listening to my prayer, and I was making progress. But recently I find myself not having too much to say. And as strange as it sounds, I don't *want* to say anything. I just want to sit there and do nothing. What am I doing wrong?"

It quickly became apparent to me that God was inviting Peter into a more meditative or contemplative style of prayer. This is the natural growth and movement from kataphatic prayer to apophatic prayer that I mentioned in Chapter 8.

"The Pure, Loving Gaze"

It's a common phenomenon: the more we pray, the less we say. And the less we say, the more the Spirit can shape and transform our prayer (see Romans 8:26). Our relationship with God is like any other relationship: the more time we spend with God in prayer, the less need we have to talk and the more we simply desire to be silent and attentive to the presence of the divine. "Be still, and know that I am God" (Psalm 46:10) is the Spirit's advice as we catch the fire of godly enthusiasm and develop a history of prayer time with God.

This stillness, silence, and attentiveness can lead to "the pure, loving gaze that finds God everywhere,"[16] to use the words of the seventeenth-century Carmelite Brother Lawrence of the Resurrection. Like any lover, we just lovingly bask in the presence of the beloved with no words or thoughts. This loving gaze is really the heart of meditative and contemplative prayer.

There are two popular methods of meditation and contemplation, slightly different from each other, that help facilitate the pure, loving gaze of God and are quite helpful when a person feels the call from kataphatic prayer to apophatic prayer. One is promoted by the late John Main, OSB, Laurence Freeman, OSB, and the World Community of Christian Meditation (www.wccm_usa.org). The other is promoted by the late Thomas Keating, OCSO, and Contemplative Outreach (www.contemplativeoutreach.org).

Each method suggests the use of a sacred word or mantra as a way of distancing ourselves from distractions and focusing our attention. The word or mantra should have no visual connotation or elicit from us any emotional response, since any associated meaning or feeling would distract us from our still, silent, and attentive gaze upon God.

The method taught and promoted by the World Community of Christian Meditation is as follows:

1. Sit down. Sit still and upright. Close your eyes lightly. Sit relaxed but alert. Breathe calmly and regularly.
2. Silently, interiorly begin to say a single word. They recommend the prayer-phrase MA-RA-NA-THA (the Aramaic expression, probably used in the early Christian liturgy, meaning "Our Lord, come!" or "Our Lord has come!"—see 1 Corinthians 16:22 and Revelation 22:20). Recite it as four syllables of equal length. Listen to it as you say it, gently but continuously.
3. Do not think or imagine anything—spiritual or otherwise.
4. If thoughts and images come, these are distractions at the time of meditation, so keep returning to the simple repetition of the word.
5. Meditate each morning and evening for twenty to thirty minutes.

The method taught and promoted by Contemplative Outreach is as follows:

1. Choose a sacred word as the symbol of your intention to consent to God's presence and action within. I find the word "Presence" to be most helpful. Some people use "Father," "Abba," "Jesus," "Mercy," among others.
2. Sitting comfortably and with eyes closed, settle briefly, and silently introduce the sacred word as the symbol of your consent to God's presence and action within.
3. When engaged with or distracted by your thoughts (which include body sensations, feelings, images, and reflections), return ever so gently to the sacred word.
4. At the end of the prayer period, remain in silence with eyes closed for a couple of minutes.

Note that in these methods the sacred word is used in two different ways. In meditation, the word is used with slow and gentle repetition. Like the repetition of the "Hail Mary" when praying the Rosary or the slow methodical beating of a drum, its role is to help us stay alert as we focus our attention and energies on the divine presence.

In the second method promoted by Contemplative Outreach and commonly called "Centering Prayer," the sacred word is not repeated like a mantra or slowly beaten like a drum as done in the method promoted by the World Community of Christian Meditation. Rather, it is repeated only when, inevitably distracted by thoughts or feelings, we need a nudge to return to the pure, loving gaze of God. When a distraction grabs our attention, we gently repeat the word interiorly, to "come back" to the conscious awareness of God.

Quality and Fruits

During meditation or contemplation, I am often tempted to analyze or evaluate the prayer experience. "This is great!" or "I must remember how I got here so I can return to this same interior place tomorrow" are self-reflective distractions that say nothing about the quality of my prayer period; such thoughts simply reveal that I have shifted my attention away from God and onto myself. The quality of my meditation or contemplation is exhibited only in my willingness, when distracted, to keep returning to the pure, loving gaze of God facilitated by the repetition of the mantra or the nudge of the sacred word.

"I'm so discouraged! I keep getting distracted when I'm trying to practice centering prayer," is a common complaint I hear in spiritual direction. I always remind my spiritual directees that the practice *is* returning to my pure, loving gaze of God when I catch myself being distracted. So if I am distracted one hundred times and one hundred times I have said my sacred word to nudge my attention back to God, then I have correctly practiced centering prayer one hundred times.

[T]he fruit of the Spirit is love, joy, peace, patience, kindness, generosity, faithfulness, gentleness, and self-control.

Galatians 5:22

The fruits of meditative and contemplative prayer are not experienced during the prayer period. Rather, they are manifested in our daily routine long after the prayer period has come to an end. We find ourselves—usually only in hindsight—glowing with godly enthusiasm and growing in the nine fruits of the Spirit. This awareness leads us to a deeper appreciation of how the Spirit uses our pure, loving gaze of God to transform us into the image of Christ: ". . . the Lover with his beloved, transforming the beloved in her Lover,"[17] to quote the line from John of the Cross's allegorical poem "Ascent to Mount Carmel."

■ REFLECT

1. When have you considered this type of prayer out of reach or inaccessible to you? What do you think now?

2. When have you felt the desire just to bask in God's presence without words or thoughts? What keeps you from doing so?

3. How do you think meditation and contemplation fit into Teresa of Avila's definition of prayer as a frequent heart-to-heart conversation with him by whom we know ourselves to be loved? How can a conversation between you and God occur if words are not used?

CHAPTER 15

THE JESUS PRAYER

■

The practice of the Jesus Prayer, similar to the techniques of meditation and contemplation discussed in the previous chapter, has its own unique character. Unlike meditation and contemplation that use a mantra or prayer word to focus one's pure, loving gaze upon God, the Jesus Prayer addresses Jesus by name and adds a petition. The most common version of the prayer is, "Lord Jesus Christ, Son of God, have mercy on me, a sinner."

A Brief History

The origins of the Jesus Prayer are found in the Egyptian desert of the fourth and fifth centuries. The desert fathers and mothers often repeated simple verses from Scripture to settle their hearts, focus their attention, and attain what Saint Paul calls "unceasing prayer" (see 1 Thessalonians 5:17).

Be cheerful no matter what; pray all the time; thank God no matter what happens. This is the way God wants you who belong to Christ Jesus to live.

1 Thessalonians 5:16–18, MSG

The earliest written form of the Jesus Prayer dates from the seventh century and reads, "Jesus, Son of God, have mercy on me." Other versions include "Jesus, have mercy on me, a sinner" "Jesus, mercy," and "*Kyrie Eleison.*"

The prayer became popular with the nineteenth-century Russian novel *The Way of the Pilgrim.* Hearing Paul's admonition to "pray always," a pilgrim travels in search of a method. He finds a *starets* (spiritual father) who teaches him the Jesus Prayer and a method to pray it uninterruptedly.

The prayer is also central to the plot of the 1961 international best seller *Franny and Zooey* by J. D. Salinger. This novel was instrumental in taking the prayer out of monastic circles and introducing it to people of different religious traditions.

The prayer is founded on the biblical understanding that God's name is conceived as the place of his presence, and knowledge of the name is evidence of a relationship with God (see Exodus 3:13–15). Its scriptural roots can be found in Philippians 2:11 ("Jesus Christ is Lord"), Luke 1:35 ("Son of God"), Luke 18:13 ("God, be merciful to me, a sinner!"), and Luke 18:38 ("Jesus, Son of David, have mercy on me!").

Four Attractions

Not everyone will be drawn to the Jesus Prayer. There are four attractions that are indicative that this prayer might be suitable and satisfying for you.

First, you feel an attraction to invoking the name of Jesus. Just as mentioning a lover's name brings to mind wonderful memories and leads you to an interior space of love, peace, joy, and security, so too you find the name of Jesus appealing and attractive.

Second, you have a felt desire for that transformation into the image of Christ. You want to become more Christlike and increase charity, purity, obedience, and peace in your daily life.

Third, you find other prayer practices too complicated and exhausting or too wordy. You feel the attraction to move from kataphatic prayer to apophatic prayer.

Fourth, you desire a simple, unified spiritual life. You have lost the attraction to gobble up spiritual books on prayer. You want to *experience* Jesus, not just read about him.

Method

There are three traditional levels to the practice of the Jesus Prayer. One begins by *verbalizing* the prayer aloud or at least moving the lips. The prayer is slowly repeated, at first 3,000 times, then 6,000 times, then 12,000 times, and then continually without counting. A woolen prayer rope, called a *chotki*, tied with 33, 50, or 100 knots, can be an aid to attention as the prayer is repeated on each knot.

Some people find it helpful to coordinate the breath with the prayer. One inhales, "Lord, Jesus Christ." One pauses with "Son of the Living God." One exhales "Have mercy on me, a sinner."

The second level of the practice is *mental prayer.* After some practice, the prayer is silent and only repeated in the mind.

The Jesus Prayer blossoms with the third level when it becomes the *prayer of the heart*. In this final stage, the prayer becomes planted in the heart and is automatically prayed with the beating of one's heart, both while awake and asleep. Prayer and pray-er are united as the prayer is repeated unconsciously. The Jesus Prayer becomes like music always playing in the background of one's life.

The genius of this simple prayer is its adaptability to various spiritual states. When we need assurance that Jesus oversees our entire lives, we stress the word "Lord." When we need to appeal to his human nature for understanding our struggles and shortcomings, we stress the name "Jesus." When we want to acknowledge his ministry as Messiah and mediator between ourselves and the Father, we stress the word "Christ." We recognize his relationship and unity with the Father when we stress the words "Son of God." When we have a specific, urgent need for mercy and compassion, we stress "have mercy on me" while stressing "a sinner" highlights a particular need for forgiveness.

Thirteen Suggestions

In a 2017 lecture entitled "The Jesus Prayer for Beginners" and posted on YouTube, the Very Reverend Protopresbyter Fr. Maxym Lysack, pastor of Christ the Saviour Orthodox Church in Ottawa, Ontario, makes some wise observations for those who want to begin the practice of the Jesus Prayer. Some of his observations go against the traditional practice of the prayer. They are worth enumerating.

1. Be modest with the amount of time you begin with. Three to five minutes are sufficient.

2. Using a prayer rope can be helpful but it's not obligatory.

3. Don't rush. Pray slowly. Don't be concerned or count the number of times you pray the Jesus Prayer.

4. It's recommended, but not mandatory, to unite the prayer to breathing because it roots the prayer deeply in your soul and body. However, overemphasizing breathing can be a hindrance and cause hyperventilation.

5. Remember you are addressing a *person* and Christ is relating to you. The Jesus Prayer is not a mantra or a method for relaxation. It might help you to relax but that's not the primary purpose of the prayer. It is intensely personal because you are addressing Jesus by name.

6. Consider starting your prayer time with the Jesus Prayer by reciting some liturgical prayers or a Psalm. This helps to "wake up" the heart and gets you ready. Do not dive into the Jesus Prayer without some preparation.

7. Don't deliberately or actively visualize anything or use your imagination. Visualization is not a part of the Jesus Prayer.

8. Don't expect instant peace and quiet. You might hear some interior noise after you start because our hearts are filled with noise. It's not a bad thing to hear that noise and it's certainly

not a reason to give up. Accept the noise and persevere with the knowledge that the noise will quiet down the more you pray the Jesus Prayer.

9. Understand that the heart is both competent to pray and wounded. Sins and passions come out of the heart, making it at times dysfunctional. But the heart, wounded as it is, was made by God to pray and to have direct, unmediated communion with God. Keep this in mind as an encouragement in prayer.

10. Prayer is a grace and gift of the Holy Spirit. It can be a challenge to fight distractions, thoughts, and images that appear instantly and multiply suddenly. We need to ask the Spirit's help when we pray. What we discover when we practice the Jesus Prayer is that the Holy Spirit is already praying within our hearts and we are trying to draw our prayer toward the Spirit's prayer and unite them into one. We occasionally feel the sweetness of the Spirit's presence and have done nothing to deserve it.

11. If you are praying the Jesus Prayer and have a strange or odd experience, consult your spiritual director. The journey to the heart is not always easy and pleasant. Because we are wounded human beings, we can be tempted with inappropriate passions as we pray. In some cases, you might have to stop the Jesus Prayer and use another method or technique.

12. The practice of the Jesus Prayer does not exempt anyone from the liturgical life of the Church and her sacraments. The two go hand-in-hand.

13. Allow the Holy Spirit to lead you to silence. If you feel the Spirit leading you to a deeper place where the prayer seems to disappear, follow the Spirit. That deeper place is a loaded silence filled with spiritual fruit.

Patrick's Eucharistic Adoration

Forty-five-year-old Patrick is a husband and father of three children. He has a full-time job as an administrator at a local university.

Every Saturday morning, Patrick drives one and a half hours to a local nursing home. He makes a point of getting there right before noon so he can have lunch with his college roommate, Nolin. Unfortunately, Nolin has no idea who this stranger is because Nolin suffers from early onset Alzheimer's disease.

Even with all his responsibilities and weekly visits to Nolin, every Wednesday morning at 2 a.m., Patrick gets out of bed, throws cold water on his face, brushes his teeth, and heads to his local parish for an hour of Eucharistic adoration.

Arriving before the Real Presence of Jesus in the Eucharist, he kneels. He begins his hour with prayers of thanksgiving for the events of the past week. He also mentions those people for whom he has promised to pray.

Having prayed prayers of thanksgiving and intercession, he sits in the pew. Once he has settled in and become comfortable, he closes his eyes and slowly recites the Jesus Prayer. As he prays it, he is consciously mindful that he is in the presence of Jesus. At times, he opens his eyes and glances at the Blessed Sacrament to reinforce his awareness of the Real Presence. He then closes his eyes again and slowly continues calling Jesus by name.

Sometimes, he feels moved to silence. And so he momentarily stops the recitation of the Jesus Prayer and simply basks in the glow of the Real Presence. "At times, I feel as if Jesus is stirring the embers in my heart," he once confided to me. At other times, he simply listens to Jesus whispering his name. "A couple of years ago, I was surprised to discover Jesus has a special name for me," he said without revealing his Jesus-given name. When Patrick finds his mind wandering off with distractions, he returns to the slow recitation of the Jesus Prayer.

As his hour comes to an end, Patrick kneels and renews his commitment to respond to whatever Jesus asks of him during the upcoming week. He concludes his hour with Jesus by slowly reciting the Our Father.

I once asked Patrick, "With so many responsibilities as husband, father, college administrator, and your weekly Holy Hour on Wednesday mornings, why on earth do you make that three-hour round trip on your day off to have lunch with someone who doesn't even recognize you?"

I saw the disappointment in Patrick's eyes. "It's the mission I receive every Wednesday morning as I sit with Jesus, call him by name, and hear him call me."

Patrick is not simply adoring the Real Presence of Jesus in the Eucharist. By being in Jesus's presence and calling him by name, Patrick is being transformed into the living flame of love. His Eucharistic adoration leads him to Eucharistic action.

The Jesus Prayer is an ancient, hallowed method of prayer. By addressing Jesus by name, we show not only our desire to deepen our relationship with him but also our willingness to be open to spiritual transformation. In the process of catching fire and becoming flame, we like Patrick are sent on mission to lovingly respond to those in need.

■ REFLECT

1. When have you felt the desire to say the name of Jesus? Were you aware that is an ancient form of prayer?
2. When have you felt any of the four attractions traditionally associated with the Jesus Prayer? How did you respond?
3. When your practice of the Jesus Prayer moves you to silence, what name do you hear Jesus calling you?

CHAPTER 16

LECTIO DIVINA

∎

On the evening of the second Sunday of every month, about one hundred Catholics in Toronto gather at St. Michael's Cathedral. After the celebration of evening prayer, Thomas Collins, the cardinal archbishop of Toronto, leads the gathered congregation in a forty-five-minute practice of *lectio divina*, the sacred reading of Scripture. Cardinal Collins initiated this devotional practice in his cathedral in response to Pope Benedict XVI's statement in September 2005: "If [lectio divina] is effectively promoted, this practice will bring to the Church—I am convinced of it—a new spiritual springtime."[18]

What Is Lectio Divina?

Lectio divina is the ancient practice of praying with Scripture. Its roots date back as far as the sixth century. It is not "reading" Scripture for information but rather "submitting" to it for transformation. Its basic premise is that God has a burning desire to be in a relationship with us, and Scripture is God's living love letter personally addressed to each one of us. If we allow ourselves to be vulnerable before this living word of love, the Spirit will use the practice of lectio divina to help us catch the fire of godly enthusiasm and mold us into the image of Christ.

Traditionally, lectio divina has been practiced privately, though nowadays, such as in Toronto's cathedral or, in my case, with a group of five friars every week, group practice is gaining popularity. By the late twelfth century, the practice was systematized into the following four steps:

Read. We begin this method of prayer with the slow, attentive, and prayerful reading of a selected Scripture passage. The passage is typically read three or four times to give a sense of the flow and content of the passage. Reading a commentary or the footnotes concerning the passage beforehand can help us understand the selected passage. Some writers like to refer to lectio divina as "feasting on the Word" and compare this first step to taking a bite.

Meditate. The second step of this feast is to "chew" the selected Scripture passage. We reflect upon each word or phrase of this love letter. We ponder its meaning and consider its implications for our own spiritual and moral lives. We brood over the words and mull over how they might be challenging us to change our behavior or attitudes to become more like Christ, or how to lovingly respond to our neighbor. Like any other word spoken in love, Scripture can sometimes be more unsettling than comforting.

Pray. Feasting on Scripture continues with savoring its essence. We engage God in conversation about our thoughts, feelings, and reactions to God's love letter. As the word comes forth from the heart of God, so our prayer arises from the heart. Since prayer is essentially a dialogue, we allow time for God to respond to our prayer of thanksgiving, praise, pardon, petition, or intercession.

Contemplate. The final step of the divine reading is to digest what we have heard and let it become a part of our body and lives. "Let the word of Christ dwell in you richly" (Colossians 3:16). As we allow God to respond to our prayer, we sit in silent, grateful love and bask in God's fiery passion that is revealed in Scripture. Here we willingly submit to the Spirit's transformative process of molding us into the Word made flesh.

Some contemporary spiritual writers like to make explicit a fifth step: *Act.* Having encountered and been nourished by God's love letter, we now continue in the banquet hall of life with new attitudes and behaviors befitting our vocation as Christians. We have not authentically encountered and submitted to Scripture without a renewed godly enthusiasm or changed behavior.

An Alternative Method

Cardinal Collins of Toronto offers those who attend his monthly lectio divina in the cathedral an alternative way of engaging in this ancient practice of Scripture reading. After a slow, attentive, and prayerful reading of the passage three times, he encourages those present to ask themselves three questions:

What is the passage saying to my head? What does this word say about God's yearning to be in a relationship with me? Scripture gives me knowledge about God and about how God looks upon me as a beloved child. I pause and ponder the divine revelation in the sacred text.

What is the passage saying to my heart? What emotions does this word incite and draw out of me? Though I might feel convicted (and need to change) or even elated by Scripture, nevertheless, I am moved to love and adore this God of unconditional love.

Today, if you hear his voice, do not harden your hearts.

Hebrews 4:7

What is the passage saying to my hands? In what ways is this passage calling me to serve God? More than simply a method of prayer, lectio divina also calls me in numerous and varied ways to lovingly respond to the unmet need or required duty of the present moment.

I have personally found Cardinal Collins's approach to lectio divina helpful in putting on the mind of Christ and following through with action. His three questions highlight Scripture's engagement and influence over my entire being. The practice of divine reading is not just gaining head knowledge, learning where passages are found in the Bible, or even memorizing verses. It goes deeper, allowing Scripture to probe, touch, and move me. My vulnerability and Christlike response show the transformative power of the Spirit and the timeless potential for the Word to become flesh again.

Paintings and Icons

There is a third method of lectio divina that is especially appropriate for prayer that engages religious art, such as paintings and icons. It's sometimes called *visio divina*, divine seeing. In her second letter to Agnes of Prague, the thirteenth-century Franciscan Clare of Assisi offered some advice about how to look upon the body of Christ on a crucifix. She wrote, "[G]aze [on him], consider [him], contemplate [him], as you desire to imitate him."[19]

We begin by *gazing* upon the figures depicted in the work and their details. We note the expressions on the faces, their gestures, the composition's symmetry or lack of it, the interplay of light and shadows, and other artistic details.

After we have studied the portrayal of the scene or person, we *consider* the motivation and intention of the artist: What is the artist saying to us in this depiction? How does the artist convey this meaning? What is striking about this depiction? What is missing or added to the customary depiction of this scene or person?

As we ponder the answers to these questions, we find ourselves growing silent as the message of the artwork emerges. This leads us to *contemplation*, where we bask in the artist's visual representation of the scriptural passage or personage.

Ideally this concludes with our deeper desire to *imitate* the Christlike qualities or virtues associated with the artwork's message.

The practice of lectio divina and visio divina remind us that Scripture and important works of art help us catch the fire of godly enthusiasm and are used by the Spirit to transform us into the image of Christ.

■ REFLECT

1. What role do Scripture and religious works of art play in your own prayer life? How have they helped you to grow spiritually?
2. What does it mean to "submit" to Scripture? How do you know when you are doing this authentically? What makes it difficult?
3. Which method of lectio divina has the greatest potential to touch and transform you?

CHAPTER 17

IMAGINATIVE PRAYER

■

I've already mentioned six prayer methods that help us respond to the ardor of God's love and catch fire: the Examen, meditation and contemplation, the Jesus Prayer, lectio divina, and visio divina. There are still others to choose from, practice, and see if you find them helpful. Each in its own unique way helps to facilitate the Spirit's communal process of transforming us into the image of Christ sent to lovingly respond to the unmet need or required duty of the present moment.

Indeed, the word of God is living and active, sharper than any two-edged sword, piercing until it divides soul from spirit, joints from marrow; it is able to judge the thoughts and intentions of the heart.

Hebrews 4:12

One of these methods of prayer uses the mind's eye to harness the power of Scripture. Sometimes called Ignatian contemplation, imaginative prayer, or composition of place, it engages our imagination—our senses, emotions, and intellects—to make us present as Jesus ministers to people in different Gospel narratives. As we enter and experience a particular Gospel scene, the Spirit can ignite the fire of godly enthusiasm.

The Method

This method of prayer has nine basic steps.

1. Begin by choosing a Gospel story. It could focus on someone in need of a healing, a miracle of Jesus, a question posed by the apostles, or a time when Jesus was alone in prayer.

2. Say a prayer to the Holy Spirit asking for help and guidance as you enter the scene. Pray for the grace to be open in whatever way the Spirit desires for the sake of your transformation. Pray also for the wisdom and courage to selflessly respond to the promptings of the Spirit during this prayer time.

3. Slowly and meditatively read the Gospel passage two or three times. You want to become familiar with the people involved, the sentiments expressed, and the plot and flow of the story. Reading the footnotes associated with the scene or a biblical commentary about it can prove helpful in understanding the scene.

4. Once you are familiar with the story, close your eyes, and, using your imagination, "compose the place." Reconstruct the entire scene. Start with the weather and the physical location. What are they like? Consciously engage all five of your senses to fully experience the story. What are the smells and sounds? Picture Jesus. What does he look like, how is he dressed, and what emotions do his actions convey? Picture the disciples and those who follow Jesus. What are they like, how are they dressed, and how are they responding? Imagine everyone involved in the plot of this Gospel story and note their actions and reactions.

5. Put yourself in the scene. Where do you find yourself in the story? Are you an idle bystander watching what is happening, or are you an active participant in the story? How are you dressed? How are you reacting and responding? What are your feelings?

6. After you reconstruct the entire scene and have found your place in it, allow the plot to play out. Is it as described in the Gospel passage, or are there twists and turns not found in the Gospel but which your imagination includes? As the plot plays out, note your emotional reactions and intellectual insights. This is the central part of imaginative prayer, so allow as much time as you need with it.

7. Gradually move from the biblical story to your own life. Freely associate the entire Gospel story with your own experience, and notice what the Spirit prompts you to remember, reconsider, or reflect upon. Do the story and plot remind you of anything in your life, past or present? For example, the raising of Lazarus might call you to consider a relationship that you thought was dead in your life but has recently reemerged in a surprising new way. The woman caught in adultery might speak to you of your own infidelities. The story of blind Bartimaeus might tap into your own deep desire to gain a new perspective or to see an event or circumstance in a whole new way.

8. Upon completing the imaginative prayer, ask yourself how you plan on actively responding to this period of prayer. Will you walk away with gratitude, with knowing that you need to seek forgiveness from someone or offer forgiveness to someone, with the challenge of living with greater faith and trust? This is where we need to listen to the promptings of the Spirit and how the Spirit wants to transform our thoughts, feelings, or actions.

9. Conclude this period of time with an appropriate prayer. It might incorporate praise, thanksgiving, petition, forgiveness, or intercession.

Some people like me do not have active imaginations. But we can still mull over the scene and reflect upon how the plot might help us catch the fire of godly enthusiasm in our lives. As Douglas J. Leonhardt, SJ, wisely notes, "Vividness is not a criterion for the effectiveness of this kind of prayer. *Engagement is* and the result is a more interior knowledge of Jesus."[20] And so we engage the story in whatever way we are able.

I have often tried to get in the boat with the disciples and be with them as they are tossed about by the storm at sea (see Matthew 14:22–33). That's a challenge for me since I don't have an active imagination and I can count on one hand the number of times I've been in a boat in my entire life. Even though nature and experience haven't given me much imaginative and sensory material to work with, I still find great light and warmth in this Gospel passage—it's been my favorite for years! As Jesus comes to the disciples walking on the water and is mistaken to be a ghost, I think back on the many times that I've been in an emotional storm—Dad's suicide, vocational crises, my departure from China as a missionary—and how Jesus came to strengthen me though I initially didn't recognize him. Watching Peter leave the security of the boat and do the impossible by walking on water gets me reminiscing about how I too was called beyond my comfort zone and asked to do what I thought was the seemingly impossible. Jesus's stretching out his hand to a sinking Peter with his admonition, "You of little faith, why did you doubt?", as he brings him back to the boat chides me to always remember that even the thinnest thread of faith can get me through the rough times. This story has often illuminated the dark periods of my life.

A Typical Reservation

Every now and then at one of my spirituality workshops, someone asks me, "If I am using my imagination, then this is all fantasy, correct? How can the Spirit transform me if all of this is just made up in my head?" These are valid and important questions.

As twenty-first-century Christians, we are coming to learn more and more about the powerful influence of the mind on our lives. Our thoughts can have a profound influence on our desires, passions, and actions, as I mentioned in chapter 5. God delights in using all our faculties—intellectual, emotional, and sensual—to satisfy the longing to be in a relationship with us. No aspect of our human nature, be it our intellectual insights, our emotions, or our imaginations, is unreachable and hidden from the grace of God.

So, if we believe in God, we also should believe that God can use every part of us—including our imaginations—to help us come to know him better. Imaginative prayer unleashes our creativity and allows the Spirit free rein to touch our lives in a unique way. Through interacting with the stories of Jesus, we can catch the fire that should be blazing in the heart of every Christian.

■ REFLECT

1. What Gospel stories might you turn to first? When and how have they been a source of comfort, consolation, or challenge for you in the past?
2. In what areas of your life could imaginative prayer provide a healing balm? A consolation? A challenge? What would be the appropriate Gospel passages to use?
3. How do you currently experience the continuing ministry of Jesus? In what ways is his ministry in the twenty-first century—including in your own life—similar to his ministry in first-century Galilee and Judea?

CHAPTER 18

WONDER-ING WITH CREATION

■

I remember taking a walk along the beach of Lake Michigan with six-year-old Jackie. She would occasionally stop, push her toes into the wet sand, and wait for the waves to wash over her feet. And then she would giggle. She encouraged me to do the same, but I refused, thinking such playful gestures foolish. A little bit later, she stopped and stared over the lake toward the horizon.

Wanting to continue walking, I impatiently asked her, "Where are you, Jackie?"

"I'm following the angel across the water to heaven," she replied.

I momentarily paused. I looked at Lake Michigan and followed it to the horizon. I didn't see any angel. As a matter of fact, I didn't see anything worth noticing or stopping for. *What is she talking about?* I asked myself.

And then I realized that Jackie still had her God-given sight, and I reflectively and regrettably wondered when I had lost my spiritual vision.

The Footprints of God

One of the unique gifts that Franciscan spirituality offers is a pair of glasses through which we can look at creation as a ladder to God. From the Franciscan perspective, God the Creator has left behind footprints in creation, and when we gaze upon this created masterpiece with the eyes of a child, we can follow those footprints as if walking up the rungs of a ladder into the divine presence. In his *Canticle of Creatures*, Francis of Assisi celebrates the majesty and reflection of God in the sun, moon, stars, wind, water, fire, and earth. The saint's first biographer, Thomas of Celano, writes explicitly about the saint, "In every work of the artist he praised the Artist; whatever he found in the things made he referred to the Maker. . . . Through his footprints impressed upon things he followed the Beloved everywhere; he made for himself from all things a ladder by which to come even to his throne."[21]

The treasures on earth boldly proclaim the Treasure above. Childlike eyes fixed firmly on earth are gradually lifted up in a spiritual direction toward heaven. With little Jackie, if we maintain or rediscover our ability to wonder at the world around us, we can be led by the angel across Lake Michigan, beyond the horizon, all the way to God.

Scripture and Tradition

"I'm not so sure I am comfortable with that. It sounds a bit pagan, like you're equating God with created things," a spiritual directee admitted to me. I reminded her that Scripture and the spiritual tradition certainly attest to the reflection of God in creation. The Wisdom of Solomon states, "For from the greatness and beauty of created things comes a corresponding perception of their Creator" (13:5). And Paul reminds the Romans, "Ever since the creation of the world [God's] eternal power and divine nature, invisible though they are, have been understood and seen through the things he has made" (1:20).

The spiritual tradition also points to God's reflection in creation. The twelfth-century Benedictine reformer Bernard of Clairvaux preached, "You will find something more in woods than in books. Trees and stones will teach you that which you can never learn from masters."[22] The fourteenth-century Dominican mystic Meister Eckhart famously preached, "A man who knew nothing but creatures would never need to attend to any sermons, for every creature is full of God and is a book."[23]

Awareness and Attention

I think we all once possessed the ability to climb the ladder of creation. But, sadly, as we grew up, most of us lost the wonder of a child. Utility replaced playfulness as we began to see a source of paper instead of a tree to climb. As we "matured," we lost our stride and the ability to walk in the footprints left behind by God, up the ladder of creation into the divine presence.

We've also lost the ability to read the book of creation. Once the source of wonder and awe, creation has now become opaque gibberish or illegible hieroglyphics. For some, it has even become a distraction that diverts their attention from the divine. What had once come naturally must now be done intentionally.

Some years ago, while preaching in northern Michigan, I had a chance encounter with a Catholic Native American named Charlie. He taught me a simple fourfold technique that many have found helpful in once again following the footprints of God with eagerness and enthusiasm. I sometimes refer to Charlie's technique as the "four A's."

"Where are you?" Charlie asked.

I was taken aback by this question. But Charlie reminded me that it's the first recorded question of God in the Bible (Genesis 3:9). I also remember it being the very question I asked little Jackie on the beach of Lake Michigan.

"It's an important question," Charlie continued, "because most of us live with a form of amnesia, completely unaware of where we really are. And so we start right here, right now, becoming conscious of where we are."

I wasn't sure what he meant, so I asked him to explain.

"It's about learning to be in the present moment. And though we hear so much about that, few know how to do it. It's quite simple. Since the senses tell us where we are, we must practice seeing what we see, smelling the odors around us, feeling what we are holding, tasting what we are eating, and hearing the sounds of the symphony that is playing around us. This is awareness, and it tells us exactly where we are and what we are doing."

Once we become *aware* of the present moment, Charlie said we must then *attend* to it. This is really the practice of deliberate attention to what our senses are registering. In this second step, we intentionally focus upon the object of one of our senses. It's one thing to see the sun setting out of the corner of our eyes; it's a whole different experience to be attentive to today's sun's final bow choreographed by the clouds and birds. It's a common experience to see a bumblebee flit from flower to flower, but how many times have we watched the way it hovers and lands? And how about a mountain spring: do we feel and taste its pristine beauty?

Assessment and Adoration

"After you have become aware of where you are and have attended to the sumptuous banquet of the present moment," Charlie said, "you then reflect upon it and *assess* what it says about God, God's goodness, God's power, and God's presence. Everything in creation points to the Creator just as every sculpture mirrors the soul of the sculptor. In that way, everything, from giraffes to gardenias, says something about God and brings us to God.

"So become aware, experience, and think about the present moment before which you stand. Thomas Merton said that a tree gives glory to God just by being a tree. If we could take the time to pause, study a tree, and reflect upon it, we could get caught up in its prayer of praise to the Creator. And that would bring us a conscious awareness of God's loving presence.

"And once we come to that conscious awareness," Charlie concluded, "like Moses before the burning bush, we take off our shoes and bow in adoration. After all, God's presence always leads us to prayer."

I instantly saw the wisdom of Charlie's process of awareness, attention, assessment, and adoration. That evening, as I drove to church, I found myself stopped at a traffic light. Out of the corner of my eye, I saw a bald eagle float against the sky. Still mulling over my conversation with Charlie, I turned the radio off and deliberately focused my attention on the bird. I carefully watched the carefree flight of the eagle. And suddenly, as the light turned green and I was on my way, I was moved to gratitude and adoration as I remembered the words of God, "I bore you on eagles' wings and brought you to myself" (Exodus 19:4).

Consider the ravens: they neither sow nor reap, they have neither storehouse nor barn, and yet God feeds them. Of how much more value are you than the birds! ... Consider the lilies, how they grow: they neither toil nor spin; yet I tell you, even Solomon in all his glory was not clothed like one of these. But if God so clothes the grass of the field, which is alive today and tomorrow is thrown into the oven, how much more will he clothe you— you of little faith!

Luke 12:24, 27–28

▪ REFLECT

1. When do you experience the childlike characteristics of wonder and awe in your everyday life? Why do you find yourself resisting them?

2. Spend some time right now right where you are, practicing the fourfold technique of awareness, attention, assessment, and adoration. Then ask: What does it teach me about myself and my location? How can I incorporate this spiritual practice into my daily life?

3. Spend time praying the first five verses of Psalm 8. Then ask: When did I last experience the wonder and awe it celebrates?

CHAPTER 19

PRAYING THE STATIONS OF THE CROSS

■

Catching fire and becoming more Christlike demands a radical identification with Jesus. My own Franciscan tradition places a distinctive emphasis upon it. And nowhere do I find that more challenging than in identifying with the sufferings of Jesus in his passion and death.

The Catholic tradition offers an ancient prayer practice that many people including me find helpful in identifying with the sufferings of Christ. It's referred to as making or praying the Stations of the Cross. Let me tell you about a unique twist that my friend Sandra brings to it.

Sandra knows that some parishioners like to pray the Stations of the Cross in the parish church on the Fridays of Lent at 7 p.m. She often joins them. She also prays them year-round.

Sandra believes that praying the Stations of the Cross is more than a mere commemoration of Jesus's final hours on earth; it involves entering and experiencing a transformative process of accepting and surrendering to the cross in her own life. Her cross is debilitating arthritis—and the disappointment that her grandchildren are not currently practicing their faith. When Friday arrives, Sandra knows, as she prays the Stations of the Cross, that it's time once again to allow the Holy Spirit to shape and mold her into the image of Christ through forgiveness, love, and patience.

A Short History

The Stations of the Cross find their origins in the Holy Land, where pilgrims desired to visit the places made sacred by the presence of Jesus. Around the fifth century, aware that not everyone could visit Jerusalem, an Italian bishop erected a group of connecting chapels that called to mind some important shrines in Jerusalem. One could now follow Christ in his passion without having to travel to Jerusalem.

During the 1400s and 1500s, the Franciscans built upon this idea, constructing small outdoor shrines across Europe that commemorated various "stations" or stopping places along Jerusalem's Via Dolorosa. Having received papal permission to erect such stations in their own churches in the late seventeenth century, by 1831 the Franciscans held the right to promote the erection of fourteen specific stations in any church as long as the parish priest received permission from his local bishop. And then by 1862 every bishop was given the right to erect stations in any church of his diocese without the intervention of a Franciscan.

Sandra's practice of praying the traditional fourteen Stations of the Cross every Friday steeps her in this rich historical tradition. However, she brings to the devotion her own twist, which helps fire her enthusiasm for God. Though this method of prayer traditionally calls us to reflect upon moments in Jesus's final hours, Sandra challenges herself to look at each station in Jesus's life and ask how she sees *herself* reflected in it. In doing this, she again becomes aware that the Spirit wants to transform her into the image of Christ. And so the Via Dolorosa of Jesus sends her toward the cross and tomb in her own life.

The Traditional Fourteen Stations and Sandra's Questions

As Sandra meditatively stands before the painting, carving, or image hanging on the walls of the church that depicts a station, she prays and then asks herself different questions. Here are the traditional fourteen stations and the questions she asks:

1. *Jesus is condemned to death.* How do I respond to unjust accusations? How does the emotional need to defend my ego manifest itself in difficult times?

2. *Jesus takes up his cross.* How do I accept the crosses in my life? How can I willingly embrace them and not actively resist them?

3. *Jesus falls the first time.* How do I respond to the weaknesses of my human nature? When and how have frailty and vulnerability been a blessing in the process of my spiritual transformation?

4. *Jesus meets his mother on the way to Golgotha.* How do I endure the sufferings and heartaches of those I cherish and love? How does my compassionate suffering with others express itself?

5. *Simon of Cyrene helps Jesus carry his cross.* When have I reached out a helping hand to others? How do I lighten the burdens of loved ones and strangers?

6. *Veronica wipes the face of Jesus.* Who bears the imprint of Jesus's bloody face in my life? How am I called to wipe away the tears, fears, and frustrations of prisoners, the homeless, delinquent children, marginalized family members, and friends?

7. *Jesus falls the second time.* When have weaknesses and struggles pulled me down? How does the Spirit come to my aid in times of sadness and depression?

8. *Jesus meets the women of Jerusalem.* How have I learned compassion in my own moments of passion and suffering? In what ways do my disappointments and suffering influence the way I respond to others?

> May I never boast of anything except the cross of our Lord Jesus Christ, by which the world has been crucified to me, and I to the world. . . . From now on, let no one make trouble for me; for I carry the marks of Jesus branded on my body.
>
> Galatians 6:14, 17

9. *Jesus falls the third time.* What moments or events in my life do I consider a failure? How did I and do I respond to them without falling into hopelessness and despair?

10. *Jesus is stripped of his garments.* In what ways have I been stripped of my emotional need for self-concern, self-image, self-gratification, and self-preservation? When do I feel painfully exposed to myself and others?

11. *Jesus is nailed to the cross.* How are anguish, affliction, and suffering transforming me into the image of Christ? When have surrender and acceptance freed me from my self-absorbed ego?

12. *Jesus dies on the cross.* Whom do I still need to forgive before I die? How do my everyday desires and daily actions reflect the way I want to die?

13. *Jesus is taken down from the cross.* What lesson has the grief of saying goodbye to a friend or loved one taught me? What does the Mother of Sorrows say to me?

14. *Jesus is laid in the tomb.* Who will come to my funeral and mourn the loss of my physical presence? How do I deal with the reality of my death?

In some churches, Sandra finds a fifteenth station: *Jesus rises from the dead.* This prompts her to ask herself: How have I experienced the Resurrection in my own life? When has the grace of God caught me off guard and totally surprised me?

The Way of the Cross in the Bible

In 2007 Pope Benedict XVI approved for public celebration a new set of stations offered by Pope John Paul II in 1991. Unlike the traditional fourteen stations, only eight of which have a specific mention in the Gospels, each of these has a scriptural reference that we can use for meditation:

1. Jesus in the Garden of Gethsemane: Matthew 26:36–41
2. Jesus is betrayed by Judas and arrested: Mark 14:43–46
3. Jesus is condemned by the Sanhedrin: Luke 22:66–71
4. Jesus is denied by Peter: Matthew 26:69–75
5. Jesus is judged by Pilate: Mark 15:1–5, 15
6. Jesus is scourged and crowned with thorns: John 19:1–3
7. Jesus takes up his cross: John 19:6, 15–17
8. Jesus is helped by Simon to carry his cross: Mark 15:21
9. Jesus meets the women of Jerusalem: Luke 23:27–31
10. Jesus is crucified: Luke 23:33–34
11. Jesus promises his kingdom to the repentant thief: Luke 23:39–43
12. Jesus entrusts Mary and John to each other: John 19:25–27
13. Jesus dies on the cross: Luke 23:44–46
14. Jesus is laid in the tomb: Matthew 27:57–60

In whatever way you do it, the practice of praying the Stations of the Cross can be a reminder that your personal cross, no matter what form it might take and no matter how or when it might appear, is one of many tools that the Spirit of God uses to transform you into the image of Christ sent to lovingly respond to the unmet need or required duty set before you. This might give you reason to join St. Paul in boasting about it in your life.

■ REFLECT

1. How would praying the Stations of the Cross help you accept and surrender to personal suffering? How would this prayer method form you into a more compassionate person?
2. What would you name as the cross or crosses in your life today? Why do you name these as "crosses"?
3. Of the fourteen stations, which one moves you the most to pause, pray, and ponder? Why?

CHAPTER 20

THE LORD'S PRAYER ANEW

∎

A while back, I discovered that the Carmelite mystic Teresa of Avila considered the Our Father a source for contemplative prayer; she even suggested that the person who takes an entire hour to pray just one Our Father will be greatly rewarded.[24] I found those statements intriguing especially since I typically pray the Lord's Prayer three times a day—but usually without much attention to what I am saying.

It was then that I took a step back and began to reconsider the meaning and importance of the Lord's Prayer in my spiritual life. I began something new: During my daily hour-long walks, I started to reflect meditatively upon the words of the prayer. Initially I would get through four or five verses of the prayer with each city block. The more I practiced this method of prayer-walking, however, the longer the spaces of silence became between the verses; I was finding more and more nuggets of meaning that were sparking into flame. I now walk an entire city block with just one verse; sometimes I am actively meditating on a particular verse while other times I am simply basking in the warmth of its fire. Though I still haven't spent an entire hour on just one Our Father as Teresa of Avila suggests, I have discovered the light emanating from this prayer. In the words of the late second-century bishop Tertullian, it truly is "a summary of the entire Gospel."[25]

What the Prayer Says about God
Our Father

The Lord's Prayer begins with the image of God as Abba, Father. This childlike image emerged early on in Jesus's life; Luke has an adolescent Jesus refer to the temple in Jerusalem as his "Father's house" (Luke 2:49). This image shaped the good news taught in Jesus's parables about God's fiery passion to be in a relationship with us: God's lavish generosity, unconditional love, and eagerness to forgive (see Matthew 6:25–34; 21:28–32; 5:45; Luke 11:5–13; 15:11– 32). It was the motivation behind Jesus's table fellowship with sinners and the marginalized. The attitudes embedded in the image of God as Abba became the benchmark for any person burning with the desire to become more Christlike: "Be perfect, therefore, as your heavenly Father is perfect" (Matthew 5:48). That image and what it represents is passed on to us as we enter an intimate relationship with the God whom the risen Christ called "my Father and your Father" (John 20:17).

Praying to "our" Father reminds us that entering this relationship with Jesus's Father is entering into a large, extended family. The process of spiritual transformation is communal. Hence, Jesus challenges us with the "greatest commandment": love of God *and* love of neighbor (Mark 12:29–31). One love complements and completes the other love. It is love of neighbor, and more importantly love of the enemy, that demonstrates our Christlikeness and the fact that we are children of the Father (see John 13:34–35; Matthew 5:44).

In Heaven

The Lord's Prayer makes clear that though God is Father, there is also a mystery about God that we will never understand or comprehend. Indeed, God dwells "in heaven," a reference Jesus pulled from the Jewish Scriptures indicating that nothing can contain the living God (see 1 Kings 8:27). And yet this mysterious, ineffable God "became flesh and lived among us" (John 1:14) in the person of Jesus of Nazareth.

Thy Name

Jewish tradition has consistently reverenced the name of God, because knowing the name is to give evidence of having an experience and relationship with God (see Exodus 3:13–15). To hallow God's name is to acknowledge not only our relationship but also what God has done in our lives: "[F]or the Mighty One has done great things for me, and holy is his name" (Luke 1:49). After the Resurrection, the early Christian community also recognized the importance and intercessory power of the very name of Jesus (see Philippians 2:9–11; Acts 3:6; 4:10–12).

Thy Kingdom Come, Thy Will Be Done

"Thy kingdom come" calls to mind the cornerstone of Jesus's good news: "The time is fulfilled, and the kingdom of God has come near; repent, and believe in the good news" (Mark 1:15). Jesus challenges us to make this kingdom the priority in our lives (see Matthew 6:33) and compares it to small, ordinary things—seed, yeast, a hidden treasure, a pearl, a fisherman's net (see Matthew 13:24–50)—to highlight how it is realized in the simplest and smallest acts of peace, love, or justice.

The realization of God's kingdom and doing the Father's will were virtually synonymous for Jesus. "My food is to do the will of him who sent me and to complete his work" (John 4:34). He referred to God's will on many occasions (see Matthew 6:10; 7:21; 18:14; Luke 22:42) and noted that our kinship in his family is based not upon blood ties but upon doing the Father's will (see Mark 3:35).

What the Prayer Says about Us

Daily Bread

The central petition of the Lord's Prayer, "Give us this day our daily bread," acknowledges that we are beggars dependent upon the alms of God, the divine almsgiver and Father. It is a call to a worry-free life and a challenge to radical trust.

> Therefore do not worry, saying, "What will we eat?" or "What will we drink?" or "What will we wear?" . . . [Y]our heavenly Father knows that you need all these things.
>
> Matthew 6:31–32

Forgive Us

We are not only beggars before God. We are also sinners in search of forgiveness for our trespasses. Jesus made clear that the Father takes the initiative to show us mercy and forgiveness like a father running down the road with open arms to welcome home a wayward son, like a woman who anxiously lights a lamp and sweeps her floor in search of a lost coin, like a shepherd who leaves a flock of ninety-nine sheep and goes in search of one lost sheep (Luke 15:1–32). In his own ministry, Jesus exhibited his Father's extraordinary sensitivity to sinners as he called a tax collector to be his disciple (Matthew 9:9–13), invited himself into the home of another tax collector (Luke 19:1–10), allowed a sinful woman to touch his body and wash his feet (Luke 7:36–50), and refused to publicly condemn a woman caught in adultery (John 8:3–11).

As We Forgive

As forgiven sinners, we are called to become torchbearers of forgiveness: "Be merciful, just as your Father is merciful" (Luke 6:36; see also Mark 11:25). Indeed, Jesus goes as far as making a direct connection between the forgiveness of our neighbor and God's forgiveness: "For if you forgive others their trespasses, your heavenly Father will also forgive you; but if you do not forgive others, neither will your Father forgive your trespasses" (Matthew 6:14–15; see also

5:7, Luke 6:37–38). Withholding forgiveness is a hypocritical form of injustice that makes us loan sharks liable for punishment (see Matthew 18:23–25).

Temptation

Jesus had experience with Satan and spoke about him on occasion (see Matthew 4:1–11; Mark 3:23–26; Luke 11:14–23; John 12:31). Our final petition in the Lord's Prayer, "Lead us not into temptation but deliver us from evil," is an acknowledgment that we need divine help to expose and refuse the conniving schemes of the devil. Sometimes misinterpreted as suggesting God might lead us into temptation, this petition is better understood as meaning, "Father, do not let us be led by ourselves, by others, or by Satan into temptations; be our savior and redeemer when we fail and sin." It reminds us that Jesus, the conqueror of evil, is the one who saves (see Matthew 1:21; John 16:33) and that, by virtue of our baptism, we have been empowered with his authority (see Luke 10:17–19).

Now and Forever

The traditional ending of the Lord's Prayer, "For the kingdom and the power and the glory are yours, now and forever," does not come from the mouth of Jesus; it was a later scribal edition to the Gospel of Matthew. However, it boldly attests to the praise and adoration due only to God the Father.

Slowly praying and meditating upon the words of the Lord's Prayer is an excellent way for glimpsing the heart and soul of Jesus and his ministry. This practice also offers us a succinct review of the worldview and lifestyle of any Christian disciple set ablaze for the glory of God.

■ REFLECT

1. In what areas of your life do the words of the Lord's Prayer challenge you daily? In what practical ways can you respond to that challenge today?

2. What does your reflection upon the words of the Lord's Prayer tell you about God? About yourself?

3. Try spending one hour in slowly praying just one Our Father. What was the experience like? What did it teach you?

Fanning

The

Flame

DISCERNMENT

As we begin to catch fire with various methods of prayer and see the light reflected in loving service, we come to know more intimately God's desires for ourselves and the world.

CHAPTER 21

DISCERNMENT OF SPIRITS

■

One evening in Las Vegas, after a long, satisfying day of presenting a workshop on the spiritual life, I was overcome with a feeling of exhilaration. A flame momentarily flared up, illuminated my entire life, and I heard myself blurt out, "I was born to teach and preach!"

Have you ever had an experience like that? Have you ever felt that you were doing exactly what you were meant to do? This is a practical way of experiencing God's spark catching fire and the satisfaction that comes in fanning its flame. It also shows that, by God's grace, you are responding to God's personal invitation to be in a relationship with him.

Figuring out that invitation—what the spiritual tradition calls "discernment"—is no easy task. It includes making important decisions as well as understanding the moods and feelings that come over us seemingly out of nowhere. Both can be confusing and are riddled with their own unique challenges, as a spiritual directee of mine recently reminded me.

Dexter faithfully practices the Examen every evening. On Wednesday or Thursday evenings, he also likes to practice lectio divina and imaginative prayer on the upcoming Sunday's second reading and Gospel. He's been quite intentional about his spiritual life for more than three years now. He once told me, "I feel like God is smoothing off all my rough edges and really shaping me into a whole new person. There are times when I just feel like I am on fire with love for God." I told him that it sounded like he was being slowly transformed into the image of Christ.

"But there are other times," he admitted, "when I get terribly confused. Something comes over me, and I suddenly lose interest in my spiritual life. I get restless, discouraged, and just want to give up. I'm not sure why that happens or what that's all about. Am I doing something wrong?"

Discernment of Spirits

Dexter, of course, is not doing anything wrong. Rather, he is experiencing the collision of two worlds. In the sixteenth century, Ignatius of Loyola, founder of the Society of Jesus (Jesuits), wrote insightfully about these two worlds and how to distinguish—discern—the difference between them.

According to Ignatius's understanding, spirits influence our spiritual lives. Some are good and some are evil. The good spirits give us consolations. Not to be confused with "feeling good," the consolation of the good spirits is really a generative and creative force that fans godly enthusiasm and gives birth to inspiration, new ideas, and enlivening energy. It makes us want to draw closer to God. It lifts us beyond ourselves and our egos and focuses our attention outside ourselves and toward others. We delight in the joys of others and feel the pain of their sorrows. It strengthens our familial and communal bonds with others. Interiorly, it keeps our most important priorities front and center as well as sharpening our vision for the things of God. As a result, the consolation of the good spirits aids us in being God-seekers and God-finders in the ordinary events of our daily lives.

Working in direct opposition to the good spirits are the evil spirits. Ignatius calls their weapon desolation. This is exactly what Dexter was dealing with in those confusing moments of his life. Sometimes confused with "feeling blue," desolation is spiritual rather than emotional. It smothers our godly enthusiasm and makes us want to give up on our spiritual commitments and practices. It turns us in on ourselves, pushing us down the steps into the dark, dank basement of self-preoccupation and negative feelings. It tries to isolate us there as hostages, cutting us off from family, friends, and community. Desolation is a heavy, dark cloud that impedes our vision and confuses us, leaving us feeling hopeless about any future with God. It tempts us to walk away from God.

Responding to the Spirits

Ignatius not only helps us discern the gift of the good spirits and the weapon of the evil spirits, but he also offers us sage advice about how to respond to consolations and desolations.

In moments of consolation, we should express our gratitude to God with prayers of praise and thanksgiving. We should place these moments in the scrapbook of our memories and periodically call them to mind and review them, especially when we later struggle against the desolation of the evil spirits. We should harness consolation's enlivening energy to fan the flames of godly enthusiasm and deepen our commitment to prayer and spiritual practices. We should also use it to stoke our selfless inspiration and willingness to be shaped by the Spirit's transformative process.

Therefore, to keep me from being too elated, a thorn was given me in the flesh, a messenger of Satan to torment me, to keep me from being too elated. Three times I appealed to the Lord about this, that it would leave me, but he said to me, "My grace is sufficient for you, for power is made perfect in weakness." So I will boast all the more gladly of my weaknesses, so that the power of Christ may dwell in me. Therefore I am content with weaknesses, insults, hardships, persecutions, and calamities for the sake of Christ; for whenever I am weak, then I am strong.

2 Corinthians 12:7–10

Moments of desolation prey upon the fickleness and frailty of our human nature. I sometimes am overwhelmed by feelings of loneliness and dejection that make me question God's abiding presence in my life. At such times Ignatius encourages us to turn to God and seek divine assistance, especially from Jesus, who can sympathize with our weakness and identify with our temptations (see Hebrews 4:15). In times of desolation, we must cling to patience; our faith tells us that God will supply us with sufficient grace to endure and emerge from these times. By deliberately seeking out friends and companions, we should intentionally work against desolation's inclination to become self-absorbed and isolated. Though it might go against the mood that overcomes us in times of desolation, it's also helpful to look for those in need and turn our attention toward them. Knowing that the fire of godly enthusiasm purifies and burns away feelings of desolation, Ignatius encourages disciples to increase their spiritual practices in these trying and dark moments. Add ten minutes to your prayer period or prolong your spiritual reading a bit. This is also the time to page through and ponder the scrapbook holding the consolations of the past. And though we might seriously consider changing decisions made during those moments of consolation, Ignatius advises that we hold our ground; moments of desolation are not the time for decision making.

The Spirit's transformative process has its ups and downs. Though the evil spirits try to hijack the process by attacking us with desolate moments, the consolations given by the good spirits help to fan the fire of God's love in our lives and give us encouragement to surrender to the Spirit's action.

■ REFLECT

1. When have you experienced consolation? How would you describe it? How did you initially respond to it?

2. When have you experienced desolation? How would you describe it? How did you initially respond to it?

3. Reflect on the difference between consolation and desolation. How will such knowledge help you to appropriately respond to each in the future?

CHAPTER 22

GOD'S WILL AND DECISION MAKING

■

Ever since I was "knee-high to a duck," as we say in New Orleans, I dreamed of being a missionary to China. I distinctly remember watching the *CBS Evening News* one day as a fifteen-year-old and having that idea glow hot again. On that particular July evening in 1970, Walter Cronkite showed a video clip of Maryknoll Bishop James Walsh walking to freedom as he crossed the Lo Wu Bridge from present-day Guangzhou (then Canton) to Hong Kong. Imprisoned for more than a decade in Shanghai, Bishop Walsh was the last and longest-held foreign clergyman to be released from prison by the Chinese Communist government.

Thirty years later while on a fact-finding mission for the Franciscan Order, I stood on that very bridge in Hong Kong and asked myself, how do I know if God is calling me to walk to the other side as a missionary?

People ask such questions when standing at a personal or professional crossroads and needing to make a decision. Posed with God in mind, the question implies the person wants the decision to be pleasing to God and according to God's plan. In effect, the question arises from the fire of godly enthusiasm—and the desire to do something about it.

God's Will, Our Gift

Many of us mistakenly think that God has a predetermined master blueprint or a detailed script for each individual life. A faithful person must figure it out, hope to get it right, and then buckle under to obey. However, such a notion smacks of the pagan idea of fate and does not respect human free will as one of the celebrated gifts of God to us.

The New Testament does state that there is a divine will and that it has been revealed: "[God] has made known to us the mystery of his will, according to his good pleasure that he set forth in Christ, as a plan for the fullness of time, to gather up all things in him, things in heaven and things on earth" (Ephesians 1:9–10). To accomplish this, God needs "co-workers for the kingdom of God" (Colossians 4:11) and "ambassadors for Christ" (2 Corinthians 5:20) who, like Christ, will find their nourishment in doing God's will (see John 4:34). In other words, God needs Christians, "little Christs."

God's urgent longing for us includes the hope and desire that we will be transformed to help with God's long-term plan. As Eugene Peterson paraphrases it, "It's in Christ that we find out who we are and what we are living for. Long before we first heard of Christ and got our hopes up, [God] had his eye on us, had designs on us for glorious living, part of the overall purpose he is working out in everything and everyone" (Ephesians 1:11–12, MSG). Our response to God's longing and the divine designs for our glorious living becomes the gift we present back to God.

Discernment

The process of deciding upon that response is what discernment is all about. As the Latin *discernere* suggests, it requires "separating off," "distinguishing," and "sifting away." What has to be separated off, distinguished, and sifted away? Our attraction and allegiance to the false self's ego-obsessions with self-concern, self-image, self-gratification, and self-preservation. To do so requires openness, self-honesty, courageous generosity, and well-aligned priorities. Once these attitudes are in place, we are then free to make the best decision that will help facilitate our transformation into the image of Christ,

Do not quench the Spirit. Do not despise the words of prophets, but test everything; hold fast to what is good; abstain from every form of evil.

1 Thessalonians 5:19–22

sent to lovingly respond to the unmet need and required duty of the present moment.

For a long time, I mistakenly believed that God would literally whisper in my ear what he wanted me to do. So I walked around with one ear up in the clouds. Now, as I approach seventy years of age, I have discovered that I need to keep my ears to the ground. "Listen to your life," as I like to tell people who attend my spirituality workshops. "Your life is a megaphone through which God is speaking and asking for your unique response to the kingdom." God's voice comes through the people we encounter, the situations in which we find ourselves, our deepest feelings, and our most creative thoughts—in the unmet need and required duty of the present moment.

There are two principal ways of discerning. Their use depends largely on an individual's personality and preference. Some of us think through a decision cerebrally, basing it on reason, good judgment, logic, and common sense. Others, like me, prefer to feel our way to a decision based upon the heart and our gut reaction to a situation. In either case, the time-tested advice for striking a balance is well worth remembering: Thinkers should "trust your head but use your gut," and feelers should "trust your gut but use your head." Discussing upcoming decisions with family, friends, and trusted confidants helps to keep that balance center stage. Discerned decisions made in secret are ill-advised and can be quite risky.

Influencing Factors

From personal experience I've learned to give ample consideration to the past, the present, my potential, my passion and desires, and my baptismal identity. That's what "listening to your life" is all about. Each of these components plays an important role in determining a personal response to God's greater will.

We are all products of our *past*. Our family and home dynamics, the values we were taught and have assimilated, and our educational experiences have left a profound impression on each one of us. Past scars and wounds might have to be addressed before the discernment process can even begin, lest we find ourselves emotionally stuck. Are today's decisions being motivated by old resentments, shames, or fears? Are these decisions more reactive than responsive to parental values or our home situation? The freer we are as we approach the discernment process, the more our response becomes a gift to God. To help facilitate that freedom, I'll discuss inner healing in chapter 29.

Our *present circumstances* present us with obligations, commitments, and responsibilities that typically need to be respected and fulfilled both today and tomorrow. Simply walking away from vows, relationships, jobs, and children could be irresponsible and downright sinful. Openness to the future comes by listening to the present moment and not ignoring our commitments to its unmet need and required duties. The future emerges from the present moment; it is not grafted onto it. Dialogue with others on this point can be extraordinarily helpful.

Our God-given talents and abilities make up our *potential*. They are clear indicators that we always remain diamonds in the rough. These natural gifts and capacities sometimes give us the opportunity to move beyond the limitations placed upon us by our past and present circumstances. They provide the wrapping paper for our unique gift and response to God.

Passion and *desires* fuel the fire in our lives and sometimes find expression in our hopes and dreams. They give us the courage to break through any fear or obstacle keeping us from the transformation by the Spirit, but they can also surreptitiously stoke the false self's ego-obsessions with self-concern, self-image, self-gratification, and self-preservation. That's why self-honesty and rightly aligned priorities are crucial when we begin the discernment process. Jesus's advice is well taken: "No one can serve two masters" (Matthew 6:24).

Some people are suspicious and distrustful of personal wishes and desires. They set up a false dichotomy between "my desires" and "God's will," thinking the two mutually contradict one another. "If I want it, it can't be of God," as Julian once said to me. Or some think that God's will is like the medicine that must taste bad to the patient.

Nothing could be further from the truth. God communicates to us through the deep attractions of our heart. A gut-level, recurring desire could very well be an invitation from God—and so we need to listen and discern from the depths of our being.

Our *baptismal identity* is a little Christ. That's who we are and who we are called to be. As we decide upon our response and gift to God in the discernment process, we allow the Word of God, especially the New Testament, to be "a lamp to [our] feet and a light for [our] path" (Psalm 119:105). The degree to which we allow ourselves to be challenged by the Scriptures and enlightened by the Church community's interpretation betrays the intensity of our godly enthusiasm. Perhaps more than anything else, our baptismal identity, which includes God's designs for our glorious living, is the woodstove of the discernment process.

It's important to remember that you should never, ever rush the discernment process. Hasty discernments can lead to harmful decisions. However, when a quick decision is called for, we pause, ponder, pray, then put one step forward, trusting God's pleasure in any decision made in good faith. Sometimes we are graced with a consolation that confirms our decision; sometimes we are not. In either case, we continue the journey with the knowledge that we walk by faith, not by sight.

My Gift to God

Knowing full well that the Lo Wu Bridge was Bishop Walsh's path to freedom, I lingered there for more than two hours as I asked, how do I know if God is calling me to be a missionary in China? That afternoon and over the next few weeks, I recalled my childhood fascination with China and seeing Bishop Walsh walk across this bridge on television. As a Franciscan friar, I knew the Franciscan Order wanted to reestablish its presence in mainland China in whatever way it could, and I believed I had the skills to learn the language and the passion to understand the culture. Walking across this bridge would give a new dimension to my preaching ministry and my Christian discipleship. My family and friends supported and encouraged my emerging decision. Feeling it was the right choice to make, I began fashioning my response to God's will by putting one foot forward and starting what would become a twelve-year journey as a missionary in mainland China.

■ REFLECT

1. How do you understand the will of God? What do you think are God's designs for using your godly enthusiasm?
2. Whom do you consult when discerning and making an important decision? Why? Which of the five elements of discernment do these people help you to consider?
3. Revisit a past decision that has proven to be unwise. What was faulty in your discernment? What information in this chapter will be helpful to keep in mind in your next discernment?

CHAPTER 23

DRYNESS, DARKNESS, OR DEPRESSION?

■

As we fan the flames of godly enthusiasm in our lives with divine help, we encounter three different realities that try to extinguish the fire in our lives. It's important to discern and differentiate these three: dryness in prayer, spiritual darkness, and clinical depression. Each is distinct and requires a different response.

Dryness

Spiritual dryness typically occurs during prayer time and is a temporary feeling of boredom, tedium, disinterest, and monotony. One's prayer is flat, sterile, cold, and uninviting. Saying prayers and reflecting upon God become hard, wearisome, and difficult to maintain. This can last for an entire day's prayer period, for a few days, or even a month or two. It is typically me-centered ("My prayer is meaningless. I'm not getting anything out of it" is the usual complaint) and fleeting, rarely lasting longer than two months.

When experiencing dryness, we often think we are doing something wrong. We think, *if I adjust my prayer technique, I could regain my momentum and again find my stride in prayer*. Such a misconception is bound to lead to frustration as we try to find that inner place where prayer used to come so easily. Dryness is a perfectly natural experience for anyone who has made the daily commitment to prayer. When we experience it, we are doing nothing wrong.

One of the great paradoxes in the spiritual life is that dryness in prayer is really an indication that something is cooking. It's a sign that the Spirit's transforming process is at work and is calling us to surrender control over our prayer techniques. We are being moved to a simpler form of prayer, one that is not so dependent on saying words or thinking and meditating upon God. This is the natural movement from kataphatic prayer to apophatic prayer that I mentioned in chapter 8.

What do we do during periods of spiritual dryness? We keep showing up; we remain faithful to our prayer time. It's easy to forget that simply showing up and going through the motions is a sign of our fidelity—and God blesses it. Rather than forcing words, we can follow the silence and sit with loving attention upon God. Slow and meditative repetition of a prayer word, mantra, or the Jesus Prayer, in sync with our breathing if that is helpful, can be an aid in maintaining our loving attention.

Darkness

Unlike dryness, which is me-centered, darkness is God-centered ("Where is God in this?" is the typical complaint). Specifically, God suddenly seems absent, disinterested, and indifferent to us. This darkness occurs after we have built a history with God and feel confident of his determination to be in a relationship with us.

Bro. Don Bisson, FMS, is a widely respected specialist in the training and supervision of spiritual directors. He wisely states that spiritual darkness happens "by evolution or revolution."[26] By evolution, he means that if we are faithful to a life of daily prayer, we will inevitably experience some form of darkness. It is a natural consequence of fidelity. By revolution, he means that we can be plunged into spiritual darkness by an event in our lives. Any form of tragedy or adversity can cause us to question the presence of God in our lives.

It's important to remember that this experience unravels, reorients, and transforms our lives. It is a radical process of unlearning. We must confront the painful question, who really is in charge of my life—my ego or God? We are forced to experience the fragility and raw reality of our weak human nature. Think of it as the dark side of grace.

The Carmelite mystic and doctor of the Church John of the Cross enumerated two "dark nights." (Contrary to popular belief, he never used the term "dark night of the soul.") The first is called the *dark night of the senses* and is likened to the pruning of branches.[27] It is characterized by a general and prolonged dryness in prayer along with the fear of being lost on the spiritual journey. We think that some sin or weakness has offended God; we are therefore being punished with God's absence. Some Christians, beset by sexual temptations and trials, wonder why these are so persistent when they keep rejecting them; some are tempted toward resentment and blaming God and think that their relationship with God is irrevocably broken; still others are racked with scruples, vocational doubts, or confusions that challenge their need to feel right with God.

It was now about noon, and darkness came over the whole land until three in the afternoon, while the sun's light failed; and the curtain of the temple was torn in two. Then Jesus, crying with a loud voice, said, "Father, into your hands I commend my spirit." Having said this, he breathed his last.

Luke 23:44–46

The God-initiated dark night of the senses, painful as it is, involving one's personal limitations, challenges and removes all one's emotional attachments to consolations and feelings of peacefulness, prayerfulness, and joy. It is a call to spiritual poverty as God nudges one not to confuse the gifts with the Giver; this confusion is often what gives rise to the need for the dark night of the senses. It is a call to surrender in faith to the mysterious God who is beyond all emotional feelings, sensibilities, and consolations.

The second darkness, the *dark night of the spirit*, is likened to the unrooting of a bush. It is undergone by relatively few people. It is a deeper and more profound experience of darkness, God's absence, and one's sinfulness than the dark night of the senses. Enveloped in the dark night of the spirit for nearly fifty years, Mother Teresa of Calcutta's admission to her spiritual director, "The place of God in my soul is blank.—There is no God in me,"[28] speaks directly to it. These people feel quite capable of committing any and every sin and are totally dependent upon God's help to avoid sin—yet God seems gone. They feel more intensely than others a lingering semblance of selfishness and sin; the few who have experienced this night, though looked upon as great saints and mystics by others, are the "worst of sinners" to themselves. During this darkness—the more profound of the two types—a person's faith, hope, and love are being radically purified while the person is challenged to live a deeper form of Christ's self-surrender and abandonment. The Spirit is transforming this person into the image of Christ found in the Garden of Gethsemane and on Calvary.

This second God-initiated darkness is a practical antidote to the most tempting form of idolatry, in which a person confuses one's images of God with the reality of God. In the dark night of the spirit, one is challenged to move beyond the natural human need to feel God's presence in the way our images of God suggest or to have God boxed in by our expectations or ideas. Like the dark night of the senses, it too is a call to spiritual poverty—but the poverty in which a person is stripped of one's beloved, trusted, and time-tested images of God. The person is called to surrender to God, who is ineffable and incomprehensible mystery.

Bro. Don Bisson cautions us from thinking of the two nights as distinct. "They form a long, natural continuum," he notes. Think of the twilight of dusk that becomes the darkness of midnight.

In these two dark nights, we are challenged to believe that God is still very much present to us—God *cannot but be present!*—but in a way that our feeble senses cannot experience, and our human minds cannot comprehend.

Depression

Unlike dryness and darkness, which are essentially spiritual in nature, depression is an emotional disturbance that finds expression in physical symptoms such as the inability to sleep or the need to oversleep; loss of physical appetite or conversely overeating; problems with concentration; lack of interest in friends, relatives, and sex; excessively low energy level; prolonged anger or irritability; reckless behavior sometimes expressed in substance abuse; headaches, chronic pain, and digestive disorders. These physical symptoms are often accompanied by negative thoughts of guilt, self-loathing, worthlessness, and, in its most extreme form, suicidal ideations. People who are experiencing dryness or darkness do not experience these characteristics as symptoms of their spiritual struggles.

In some cases, depression can be genetic or hormonal. However, in many cases, it is our reaction to an unexpected or continuing negative life event, such as financial problems, problems with significant relationships, or marriage stresses such as separation or divorce. And there's loneliness, the memory of childhood trauma or abuse, health issues or chronic physical pain, or any other unexpected event that causes undue emotional stress.

Depression makes it difficult to pray or find any consolation in one's relationship with God. As a matter of fact, depression will sometimes challenge and test one's prayer life and images of God. So it can look like dryness or spiritual darkness. But this is more a by-product of the nature of depression, especially in the religious person, and not an indication of dryness or darkness per se.

Prolonged depression, unlike the passing "blues" that we all experience on occasion, needs to be treated by a competent clinical professional. Attempts at self-diagnosis and self-medication can often only prolong the emotional pain. Professional help needs to be accompanied by social support (connecting with friends, relatives, and sometimes support groups), working on emotional skills (learning how to express emotions appropriately), lifestyle changes (getting regular rest, exercise, eating healthily, learning how to manage stress, changing negative thought patterns), and sometimes medication. Emotional stability gives us confidence for daily life.

Many of us will encounter dryness, darkness, and depression as we fan the fire of godly enthusiasm in our lives. Knowing how to distinguish between them and respond to each of them facilitates the Spirit's process of transforming us into the image of Christ.

■ REFLECT

1. When have you experienced dryness in prayer? How did you respond to it? What did it teach you about prayer?

2. How have dark periods in your life affected your relationship with God? How was your relationship with God different after the darkness faded and light returned?

3. How attached are you to your feelings in prayer? How do you pray when prayer doesn't make you feel good?

CHAPTER 24

SPIRITUAL DIRECTION

∎

I began feeling the attraction to prayer as a fifteen-year-old. I asked a priest about its meaning and how to respond to it. I started meeting with him about once a month to discuss my life and what was happening spiritually. Over the past five decades, I have continued to meet regularly with someone as I have grown in the conviction that the spiritual journey is something that we're not meant to travel alone. It truly is a communal process.

People who are serious about fanning the flame of godly enthusiasm in their lives typically find a spiritual companion who agrees to accompany them on the journey. This companion is traditionally called a spiritual director.

In one sense, the term *spiritual director* is something of a misnomer. The term suggests that the companion takes the lead, directs, and tells you what to do. But that is not the proper or traditional role of the spiritual director. As a matter of fact, seasoned spiritual directors always do more listening than talking.

The Holy Spirit and the Spiritual Companion

In another sense, the term *spiritual director* hits the nail on the head. The Christian tradition has always said that there is only one spiritual director on the spiritual journey: the Holy Spirit. The role of the spiritual companion is to help us get in touch with the Holy Spirit, discern where

If we live by the Spirit, let us also be guided by the Spirit.

Galatians 5:25

the Spirit is leading us, and encourage us to follow the promptings of the Spirit with a grateful and generous heart. Hence, the spiritual companion directs our attention—that's why he or she is called a director—to how and where the Spirit is working in our lives. The spiritual companion neither tells us what to do nor tries to convince us of his or her own approach to the spiritual life. The spiritual companion is simply present to keep our attention focused on grace and be a witness to the Holy Spirit's promptings. The spiritual director or companion offers us encouragement—and sometimes guidance in the form of suggestions—so we can fully be aware of and freely respond to the transformation by the Spirit.

As a witness and a source of encouragement, the spiritual companion holds us accountable as we name and claim God's grace in our lives. That naming and claiming provides the content of the monthly spiritual direction session, typically lasting fifty minutes, and forms the heart of the spiritual direction relationship. Together the two parties reflect on the following questions as they relate to the directee:

- *Who* has God recently been using to speak to me?
- *What* is God doing in my life right now?
- *When* have I recently been asked to take a step in faith?
- *Where* is God calling me?
- *Why* is God inviting me to embrace a certain person or a certain situation?
- *How* am I responding to God's grace and invitations?

The answers to these questions help motivate and give the directee momentum to submit to the Spirit's action. The spiritual companion will sometimes remind the directee of what he or she has already experienced and will encourage him or her to remain faithful when fear or fatigue begins to dampen the Spirit's fire.

A spiritual companion or director can be especially helpful when you are trying to discern God's call and voice. The advantages and benefits of having a spiritual director quickly come to light when you ask whether to have a child, accept a transfer to another city, or respond to an employment opportunity. A spiritual director can accompany you through periods of spiritual dryness and help you learn from seasons of grief and loss. A spiritual director can also point out stepping-stones through the turbulence caused by transition.

Some people mistakenly confuse a spiritual director with a counselor or a life coach. Each has a specific role. A counselor helps us negotiate the emotional struggles and psychological issues that often arise. A life coach teaches us techniques to maximize our time, talents, and potential. A spiritual director is a witness and source of encouragement as we begin to surrender to the Spirit's action and fan the flame of God's love. Though there might be times when a spiritual director makes suggestions that help someone manage emotional hurdles or make the most of their time and talents, the proper place for the spiritual companion is at our side as we respond to the Spirit's movements.

Personal Qualities Needed for a Spiritual Directee

Before I commit to accompanying someone on the spiritual journey, I have an initial meeting with him or her. The purpose of this meeting is for the potential directee to get a sense of my personality and approach to spiritual direction. It also gives me the opportunity to assess if the potential directee has certain qualities needed to benefit as a spiritual directee. I hold a minority view that spiritual direction is not for everyone.

What are some of the qualities that I look for in a potential spiritual directee? They include:

- The person prays regularly in a reflective style. He or she has an active relationship with God that goes beyond "saying prayers" and regular church attendance.
- The person is able to reflect upon his or her life experience and draw out meaning and sense the Spirit's movement. This quality does not have to be well developed but it should be present in some nascent form.
- The person is willing to talk about what is happening in prayer and can convey the feelings and movements that arise.
- The person knows how to trust and be vulnerable.
- The person has the desire and maturity to grow spiritually, despite the cost. This includes talking about the dark side of his or her personality.
- The person can endure ambiguity and live in an untidy mess.
- The person is mature enough to take responsibility for actions taken. The potential directee is not quick to blame or shame others.
- The person exhibits a certain level of freedom. He or she is not immediately looking for cheap therapy or grief counseling. Though therapy or counseling might be needed later in our journey together, it is not the immediate reason for starting spiritual direction.

I'm aware that not everyone possesses all these qualities. Nor do I expect them to. I've accompanied people whose lives are in moral disarray, but they are very much aware of it and are willing to work through their issues as the Spirit prompts them. A reflective spirit and openness to the Holy Spirit are crucial.

Personal Qualities of a Good Spiritual Director

What should you look for in a spiritual director? The qualities include:

- A spiritual director should first and foremost be a good listener who can keep confidentiality. After all, you'll want to be able to trust this person with your deepest experiences and emotions. A companion who is always talking, who is suspicious and critical, or who is always trying to fix a situation is not particularly helpful as a witness and source of encouragement when you are attempting to name and claim God's grace in your life.

- The director should have a wealth of life experience, especially in terms of the midlife transition, and be a person who evidences prayerful faith well lived.

- A director who is open to wonder and surprise clearly knows that God's ways are not our ways (see Isaiah 55:8). The director lets the Spirit be the Spirit in the life of the directee without condemnation, judgment, bias, or prejudice. A helpful spiritual companion allows the directee to pursue his or her own unique path to holiness.

- A good director is aware of his or her own weaknesses and strengths.

- A director should know the basic principles of discernment.

- Seasoned spiritual directors have their own spiritual directors.

- Finally, the ideal spiritual director has an adequate understanding of the faith and spiritual traditions, is informed by basic psychological principles, and has enough self-awareness to know when he or she is being more of a hindrance than a help along the journey.

Of course, no one possesses all these qualities, but many people possess a few more than others. Be aware that a spiritual director doesn't have to be a vowed religious or an ordained member of the clergy. There are many laypeople—from homemakers to businesspeople—who have been trained in the ministry of spiritual direction and who possess many of the characteristics of a good spiritual companion.

Finding a spiritual director can take a little legwork. The first place to inquire is at your local church. Many now have on-staff spiritual directors, people trained to accompany church members. Also consider inquiring at nearby convents, monasteries, retreat houses, or Christian conference centers. Many offer spiritual direction as an outreach to the wider Christian community in their area. A third resource is the free website of Spiritual Directors International at www.sdiworld.org. Clicking the top tab "Find" will lead you to their "Find a Spiritual Director/Companion Guide." After answering some basic questions and noting your location, a list of compatible and suitable spiritual directors will appear. The spiritual directors' contact phone numbers and religious denominations are listed. The website of Spiritual Directors International includes practical information and important questions to ask as you begin your search for a spiritual companion. I often encourage people to schedule an initial session with three potential directors and see who of the three makes for a comfortable and helpful match.

Know that you might not have to go to the physical location where the spiritual director resides. Since the pandemic of 2020, many spiritual companions have made the transition to offering virtual spiritual direction using online conference platforms such as Zoom, Skype, Webex, and GoToMeeting. From my friary in Texas, I've done spiritual direction with people in California, Washington, Tennessee, and New Hampshire.

People often wonder if payment is appropriate for spiritual direction. There are two opposing schools of thought on this. One says that spiritual direction is a ministry in the church, and those who have been given and called with this gift should freely offer their services (see Matthew 10:8). Traditionally one has never paid for this ministry. But nowadays, offering a stipend to spiritual directors who have invested their time and money in formal training is not unheard of. How much should you offer? I recommend your own professional hourly wage or what you consider the value of an hour of your own time as a fair donation. Most spiritual companions would never turn someone away for lack of funds to pay for spiritual direction.

Be aware that after one, two, or three years, you might outgrow your spiritual director. Having the uncanny ability to predict what your companion will say, or finding sessions unhelpful, could be a sign that it's time to move on to another director. Seasoned spiritual directors know this to be the case so you won't be hurting their feelings. Some might even be able to suggest others whom they know to be mature spiritual directors. It can be a gift both to yourself and your director if, in the final session, you mention the highlights of your journey with your spiritual companion.

In summary, what are the values and benefits of spiritual direction? It strengthens perseverance in times of spiritual discouragement and provides an avenue to name, claim, and celebrate God's grace. It encourages us to respond freely, graciously, and generously to the promptings of the Spirit as the fire of godly enthusiasm blazes in our lives.

■ REFLECT

1. Which qualities and characteristics of a spiritual director would be the most important in a person accompanying you on the spiritual journey? Why those?

2. What hesitations do you have about talking with a spiritual director? Where do you think these hesitations come from?

3. If asked today, how would you answer the questions of a spiritual director: *Who* has God recently been using to speak to me? *What* is God doing in my life right now? *When* have I recently been asked to take a step in faith? *Where* is God calling me?

CHAPTER 25

SELF-CARE AND WELLNESS

■

A Franciscan friar I knew, now deceased, once used mileage points to upgrade to first class on a flight from Los Angeles to New York. As he relaxed and sipped his glass of Scotch, the flight attendant approached and said, "Father, Mother Teresa of Calcutta is in the back of the plane, and if you don't mind, I would like to invite her to sit in this empty seat next to you."

The friar was suddenly embarrassed at being in first class and lost his taste for the Scotch. He tried his best to convince the flight attendant to leave Mother Teresa alone. Three minutes later, the flight attendant returned with Mother Teresa. "Please, Mother," the flight attendant said to her, "take this seat."

The friar blushed with shame and embarrassment as the glass of Scotch became Exhibit A, proving him guilty of a comfortable life, unbecoming a son of the poor Saint Francis.

"What can I get you to drink, Mother?" the flight attendant asked.

The friar slumped in his seat and wished he could hide the evidence in front of him.

Mother Teresa of Calcutta spied the glass of Scotch in front of the friar and replied, "I'll have a glass of red wine, please. Preferably cabernet sauvignon." And turning to the friar, she said with a twinkle in her eye and a wry smile, "Father, doctors say that red wine is so much better for the heart than what you're drinking!"

Halos and Health

Many people find it difficult to think of Mother Teresa of Calcutta drinking a glass of cabernet sauvignon in first class. That's because we often think of saints as thin, ascetic-types with dark circles under their eyes, who mutter prayers under their breath. Tough and determined with no *joie de vivre*, they surely fast daily and have little toleration for rest, relaxation, or exercise.

That was, in fact, the traditional view of holiness. However, over the centuries as our understanding of physical health, human psychology, and the spiritual life developed, so too did our understanding of what it takes to fan the flame of godly enthusiasm. We now understand halos as coming *with* a healthy lifestyle and not at the expense of it. The spiritual life is primarily *life*—and that means experiencing it in a sensible and well-balanced way, "hav[ing] it abundantly," in the words of Jesus (John 10:10).

Blessed Are the Balanced

During my four years of theological training as a priest, I decided to fast twice a week to deepen and grow spiritually. On my fast days, I committed to praying an extra hour instead of taking my daily hour-long walk. I also decided not to check my mailbox or telephone my family and friends on those days.

Within three weeks, I found myself becoming blue as Wednesday and Friday approached. On those two days, I became irritable and cranky and resented hearing laughter coming from the dining room. Hearing my reactions to my self-imposed fast from food, exercise, and companionship, my spiritual director cautioned, "When it comes to the spiritual life, overzealousness is a hindrance, not a help, Albert. Fasting and prayer should be coupled with exercise and community life and not be perceived as being in competition with them. Blessed are the balanced."

Balance is a blessing, indeed. Many of us are challenged to achieve and maintain it. We are tempted to live our lives off kilter, allowing predispositions and attractions—however noble and laudatory they might seem—to control us, neglecting our physical health, ignoring the emotional requirements of being human, sometimes even overemphasizing our relationship with God at the expense of our families and friends. That was my mistake as I thought the spiritual life was in competition with my physical and emotional needs. On life's journey, it's so easy to keep our eyes fixed on heaven above and end up bumping our heads below. It's critical to strike a healthy balance mentally, physically, emotionally, and spiritually.

Mental Stimulation. When I asked ninety-two-year-old Sr. Agnes, a cloistered nun, the secret to staying sharp as a tack, she instantly replied, "The daily crossword puzzle in the newspaper! It's one of the best ways to thank God for what's between our ears."

The brain is a muscle that needs to be exercised. The more we use it, the more we keep it in shape. Besides contemplating the daily crossword puzzle, we can read a novel, learn a foreign language (even if we never intend on using it), go to the movies, see a play, visit a museum, or spend the day at the county fair. All of these are ways to celebrate and use the gift of the mind.

People like Augustine of Hippo, Thomas Aquinas, Bonaventure, and Edith Stein also remind us that following the path of the intellect is not only a good way to exercise and thank God for the gift of the brain, but also a valid way to holiness. For some people, study is part of the spiritual process used by the Spirit to transform them into the image of Christ.

Physical Needs. Our physical bodies are also gifts to be reverenced. They require plenty of water, healthy food, adequate sleep, and proper exercise. They also need rest and relaxation. They require regular medical checkups for prevention and, sometimes, medical attention. They often show their appreciation with a delightful sigh during a vacation, during time spent vegging in front of the television, or when listening to music.

If the needs of the body are ignored, they often go underground and come out in unhealthy physical ways. Angry outbursts, overeating, drinking too much, high blood pressure, suddenly dozing off, or inappropriate sexual behavior can sometimes be symptoms that the body is in distress. We need to listen to our bodies because they never lie.

The sixth-century Rule of Saint Benedict highlights how care and respect for the body can aid our spiritual growth. Its balanced spirit is summed up in the classic Benedictine motto, *ora et labora* ("pray and work"). It legislates about six hours of daily manual labor, shows wise consideration for the food offered to sick and senior monks, and notes the importance of sleep, permitting a siesta in the summer if needed. I have often wondered if Mother Teresa of Calcutta knew that chapter 40 even allows for wine!

Heart Rates. By their very nature, emotions need to be expressed. People of godly enthusiasm know full well the importance of laughter, joy, desire, hope, sadness, fear, affection, courage, and anger. Each of these emotions needs to be recognized and expressed in an appropriate and healthy way, which might include:

When Jesus saw her weeping, and the Jews who came with her also weeping, he was greatly disturbed in spirit and deeply moved. . . . Jesus began to weep. So the Jews said, "See how he loved him!"

John 11:33, 35–36

- watching the wonder and awe of children at play
- spending intimate time with one's spouse
- writing letters to Congress
- visiting friends and relatives
- expressing gratitude and thanksgiving
- enjoying favorite television shows and movies
- giving ourselves permission to cry
- laughing heartily

- giving anger an appropriate voice
- fostering a healthy self-image by affirming, loving, and respecting oneself

In the past thirty years, contemporary psychology has been reminding us that when it comes to personal success "E.I." (Emotional Intelligence) is just as important, and maybe more so, as "I.Q." Remember, the heart rates!

High-strung by temperament, I found myself becoming emotionally disengaged within five months of arriving in mainland China. I was lonely, had lost my appetite, and was having trouble sleeping. I was also developing a distain for everything Chinese. One of the most embarrassing moments of my life occurred when, in a moment of frustration while trying to get a haircut, I blurted out, "Why doesn't anyone speak English around here?" Had I forgotten that I was in the middle of China?

That afternoon, I tried to pray in chapel and couldn't. What's going on inside of me?, I asked myself. I painfully admitted that perhaps I had made a mistake by becoming a missionary. As I reflected upon my feelings and pondered their physical manifestations, I came to the realization that I was in the throes of culture shock. The answer to my question then became kindling for my prayer to God. "O God, have I made a mistake by coming here? I'm struggling. Here's the deal: I'll stay if you provide me with the grace of your strength." Attention to my feelings gave me my daily prayer as a missionary to China for twelve years.

The twelfth-century reformer of the Benedictine Order, Bernard of Clairvaux, stressed the spiritual role of emotions and affections. His emphasis highly influenced my own Franciscan tradition. Asking oneself, *what am I feeling?*, is a great way to foster self-awareness and begin any heart-to-heart conversation with God and others.

Spiritual Desires. It's easy to overlook, think unimportant, or postpone satisfying the needs of our spirits. "I'm too busy to pray today," we often say to ourselves. But satisfying these hungers is also critical for our overall self-care and wellness. Responding daily to our spiritual desires through prayer and spiritual practices, even for ten or fifteen minutes, helps to fan the fire that the Spirit has sparked.

The mind, body, heart, and spirit are like different kinds of wood, each contributing to the burn time and intensity of a fire. Sparked by the Spirit, they ignite into the fire of godly enthusiasm and, if given our due attention, keep that fire burning both day and night.

■ REFLECT

1. Whom do you consider to be holy or saintly? What do their characteristics say about your understanding of holiness?
2. On a scale of one (dangerously off kilter) to four (balanced), how would you rate your awareness of and attention to your mind, body, heart, and spirit? Why?
3. Between your mind, body, heart, and spirit, what do you find the most difficult to be attentive to? Why?

CHAPTER 26

DEVELOPING A RULE OF LIFE

■

Joan first heard the suggestion of writing her own rule of life from a parish priest's homily. He noted that some of the great founders of religious communities—Augustine, Basil, Benedict, Francis, and Clare of Assisi—had proposed rules to their followers as a way of becoming more like Christ. He then suggested that writing a personal rule of life could serve as an encouragement and reminder of the commitments one makes to fan godly enthusiasm into flame.

Joan's curiosity was piqued. "But I have to be honest," she added in a spiritual direction session with me, "the idea of obeying an elaborate rule in my life—written by me or someone else—is a little unsettling and unrealistic."

To set Joan's mind at ease, I thought I would explain to her what a rule of life is and isn't.

The Characteristics of a Rule of Life

A rule of life is a statement about how we will be open to and help foster the process of being transformed by the Spirit of God. Specifically, it provides a structure for our approach to CPR (community, prayer, and repentance). It also expresses our commitment to the three primary relationships in our lives: God, others, and self. It proposes a manner of living that reflects our growing love for God, others, and self while respecting our own unique individuality. Far from being an elaborate and meticulous ordinance requiring dotted *i*'s and crossed *t*'s, a rule of life is more like a gardener's trellis that supports a living vine and helps it grow. It offers a rhythm for living life to the full and being open to the Spirit.

A rule of life is not an ideal we are striving to achieve, written from the shoulds and oughts of a guilty conscience, but rather the minimum standard of our lived experience. "There are certain things I do and just don't do because I am in a committed relationship," as Jerry reminded me. This kind of thinking provides the content for a realistic statement of your present circumstance and sets the benchmark for your relationships with God, others, and self for which you can honestly and truly be held accountable.

In its nuts and bolts, simply put, a rule of life is a written document. It can be of almost any length, but I find that the most effective ones fit on one page.

Every person's rule will be uniquely phrased, depending on his or her personality and life situation. The rule is meant to express your answers to some specific questions: How am I personally committed to God? In what ways? What is my unique role in the world—how will I be open to the Spirit and fan the fire of godly enthusiasm in my life?

The most realistic rules are not written in one sitting; they are written, rewritten, and tweaked over days, weeks, and months until they truly express how we are living and want to live as the image of Christ. They are living documents that, if kept in our journal, indicate how we have changed and grown in each season of life.

Before beginning to write a rule of life, it is worthwhile to ponder and pray over the following questions:

- When and where do I feel closest to God? How do I enter most deeply into a contemplative awareness of God's presence in my ordinary life? What, if any, particular practices are more helpful for me to become a God-seeker and God-finder? What spiritual practices of community life, prayer, and/or repentance (CPR) weigh me down or slow me down on the spiritual journey?

- What is most important to me? What do I really want out of life, and what's stopping me from getting it? Looking at my calendar and checkbook, who or what receives the most attention in my life? If I had only six months to live, how would I spend my time and money?

- When I reflect upon my relationships with God, others, and myself, how do I answer the following questions: What do I want to start doing? What do I want to stop doing? What do I want to continue to do with greater deliberateness and intentionality?

- How do I currently realize my goals and longings for work? For studying? For praying? For relating to significant others and friends? For networking with colleagues? For maintaining diet and exercise? For playing and recreating? Which of these activities foster or dampen the fire of godly enthusiasm for me? Which need greater attention?

- Considering the limitations in my life right now—my interior longings as well as my external responsibilities—what spiritual, relational, and educational practices suit my daily, monthly, and yearly rhythms?

- What can I change in my life? What am I powerless to change?

A Possible Structure for Your Rule of Life

After spending significant time reflecting and working through these questions, you can begin building the trellis that will become your rule of life. It's important to remember that the language used and the structure adopted are just two creative considerations that make the rule of life uniquely yours. Here's one possible structure:

- *Life Statement*: A short, concise one sentence summary of your personal spirituality. Think of it as a twenty-second elevator speech in answer to the question, "Why did God create you?" This could be a passage from Scripture, a personal mission statement, or some phrase or expression that you gravitate toward because it sums up the ideals you strive for in your relationship with God, others, and self.

When he came to Nazareth, where he had been brought up, he went to the synagogue on the Sabbath day, as was his custom. He stood up to read, and the scroll of the prophet Isaiah was given to him. He unrolled the scroll and found the place where it was written: "The Spirit of the Lord is upon me, because he has anointed me to bring good news to the poor. He has sent me to proclaim release to the captives and recovery of sight to the blind, to let the oppressed go free, to proclaim the year of the Lord's favor." And he rolled up the scroll, gave it back to the attendant, and sat down. . . . Then he began to say to them, "Today this scripture has been fulfilled in your hearing."

Luke 4:16–21

• *Preamble*: A brief three-to-four-sentence explanation of your life statement. Why is your life statement important to you? What are its practical implications in your daily life?

• *Your Relationships*: Write one or two sentences about the importance of each of your key relationships: with God, others (your significant other, your family, your wider circle of friends, your colleagues at work, and the family of creation), and yourself. If you were on your deathbed, what would you want to say to each if given the opportunity?

• *Your Commitments*: State clearly and explicitly what you will do to foster and celebrate each relationship (God, others, and self) on a daily, weekly, monthly, and yearly basis.

• *Accountability*: How will you hold yourself accountable to this rule of life? How often will you revisit it to check it, tweak it, and make sure it continues to be a living document? With whom will you be sharing it (spouse, trusted friend, spiritual director, etc.)?

An Example

Adam, forty years old, is married with two children and works as an administrator in a hospital. With his gracious permission, I share with you his rule of life, which sits in a frame on his desk at work:

As a disciple of Jesus Christ, I am committed to living out the teachings of Jesus. As a husband, I am called to make the Father's love a reality for my wife. As a father, I am committed to supporting my wife in raising our children. As a colleague and friend to many, I will live the Golden Rule both professionally and personally.

- *Discipleship: I am committed to twenty minutes of solitary prayer a day and to weekly church attendance with my family. Three times a month, I spend time meditating on Scripture and/or reading a spiritual book. Every June, I attend a weekend retreat (two overnights) with the men's club of my church.*

- *Husband: I will reverence and celebrate Laura as God's love made flesh for me. I am committed to a daily phone call to her from work, a weekly date night, and an annual vacation with her and the children. We are open, honest, and follow Ephesians 4:26–27.*

- *Father: As gifts from God, my children come before my career. I support Laura in her decisions about them and will not drive a wedge between her and them. Twice a month, I spend quality time with each one of them individually and will do my best to offer them memorable annual vacations.*

- *Colleague and Friend: I live by the Golden Rule with no exceptions. When warranted, I treat a colleague as a friend. I stay in touch with my three closest friends on a monthly basis and when possible, invite one for coffee once a month.*

- *Myself: I commit to some form of physical exercise three times a week. I also commit to splurging on myself in some way, shape, or form three times a month.*

I will share this rule with Laura. Every September, I will revisit it, revise it if necessary, and recommit to it.

In summary, a realistic rule is born from reflection upon one's present life and addresses how to create and promote a balanced, healthy lifestyle. Many people initially write a rule that is top heavy in one relationship while ignoring or neglecting others. That's why we need to rewrite and tweak it over time, making sure we are promoting a healthy interaction and balance between being/doing, prayer/action, engagement/solitude, words/silence, speaking/listening, asceticism/celebration, and body/spirit. The process of spiritual transformation that the Spirit accomplishes in us begins *right where we are* in *this* life, not another.

Second, a realistic rule of life is not a rambling litany of overcommitments or unmet ideals longing to be fulfilled. It states a person's current *lived* reality and should fit on one typed page. State what is doable and can be measured with specific, observable behaviors. A rule of life is not a straitjacket that binds but a passport to freedom, creativity, and new adventures.

As we grow into the image of Christ, we will come to view our rule of life as a mission statement that not only proclaims the grace of God in our lives but also gives us direction in setting the world on fire.

■ REFLECT

1. What do you find most challenging about writing a rule of life for yourself?

2. What difference would it make to actually write down your commitments to God, others, and self and then share them with your spouse, best friend, or spiritual director?

3. What relationships in your life do you simply let happen and not intentionally foster and promote? How would a rule of life actively strengthen awareness of those relationships?

Becoming

All

Flame

DYNAMIC COMMITMENTS

The Spirit of God energizes us with vigor and
passion that keeps the fire of godly enthusiasm
blazing in our lives.

Becoming

All

Flame

DYNAMIC COMMITMENTS

CHAPTER 27

AN EXAMINATION OF CONSCIENCE

■

God's spark catches fire in the lives of many people. You can feel its warmth in those kneeling in Eucharistic adoration chapels, serving in soup kitchens, offering loose change to beggars on the street, silently praying as they commute to work, and selflessly sacrificing for their children. That fire is fanned when these people take responsibility for their spiritual transformation by opening themselves to God's will, spiritual direction, a healthy lifestyle, and being accountable for living an intentional life of faith.

But the fire of godly enthusiasm doesn't stop there. It blazes in commitments that foster and fuel the spiritual practices I have already discussed. These commitments possess a dynamism that will serve as an important reminder: you are not only called to catch fire and be transformed into the image of Christ, but you are, in fact, designed to become all flame!

My friend Martha told me about her experience with one of those dynamic commitments, a weekend retreat.

During his first session on Friday evening, the preacher asked the forty people on retreat a simple question, "How are you doing with God?" He then began to walk them through the Ten Commandments and the Beatitudes of Jesus, asking questions after each one: "I am the Lord, your God. You shall not have strange gods before me. *What are the strange gods that I worship in life? Money? Food? Sex? My reputation?* . . . Blessed are the meek; they will inherit the earth. *How have I abused the power and authority entrusted to me by my vocation in life, my occupation, and the roles I play at home or in the community? How can I grow in the childlikeness and humility that Jesus shows to be important in the kingdom of God?"*

That first session gave Martha the impetus to go to confession—something she hadn't done in a very long time. It also introduced her to a simple method of self-reflection recommended to those who respond to the spark from God, fan godly enthusiasm in their lives, and then stoke its flame to keep it burning.

The Importance of Self-Reflection

To be shaped by the Spirit into the image of Christ, we need to become aware of the rough edges in our lives, those places where we deliberately choose to live in the darkness and selfishness of sin. Self-reflection and repentance are early and critical tasks in the Spirit's transformative process. Without the awareness of our sinfulness, we risk sabotaging the work of the Spirit.

Happy are those who do not blunder with their lips, and need not suffer remorse for sin. Happy are those whose hearts do not condemn them, and who have not given up their hope.

Sirach 14:1–2

Over the centuries, self-reflection has been promoted through the practice of an examination of conscience. Unlike the examination of consciousness ("Examen") mentioned in chapter 13, the examination of conscience is the deliberate review and analysis of our thoughts, words, and deeds—and, more importantly, their motivations—in the light of our response to God. We sift through them in a measured, meticulous, and methodical way, to be aware of the control that the false self and its ego-obsessions continue to yield over our minds and hearts. The result of such an examination is the deliberate decision to add more kindling to the fire of our godly enthusiasm.

There are numerous ways to examine one's conscience. The retreat preacher had introduced Martha to two common forms: one based on the Ten Commandments and one based on the Beatitudes. Another method involves reflection on the theological virtues of faith, hope, and charity. You'll find online versions of these three and others by googling "examination of conscience."

The Fruit of the Spirit

In the letter to the Galatians, Paul encourages us to "live by the Spirit" (5:16) and later adds, "If we live by the Spirit, let us also be guided by the Spirit" (5:25). He explicitly notes the nine "fruit of the Spirit" that are practical indications that we are living and guided by the Spirit: "love, joy, peace, patience, kindness, generosity, faithfulness, gentleness, and self-control" (5:22).

If our enthusiasm is fueled by the Spirit of God, then it's wise to ask ourselves how we obstruct, impede, and thwart the Spirit from bringing forth the divine fruit in our lives. Consequently, an examination of conscience based upon the Pauline fruit proves worthwhile and can look like this:

- *Love.* How have the wounds and grudges that I hold on to hindered me from becoming a person of love and acceptance of others, especially those who have wronged or betrayed me? In what ways have I made people pay for my attention and affection? How have I deliberately subverted the practice of the Golden Rule?

- *Joy.* How have I disrespected the gift of life and the wonders of creation that God has graciously bestowed upon me and allowed me to experience? How have my actions and attitudes sabotaged the exuberance for life and the firmly grounded hope that are rooted in the ultimate victory of Christ's resurrection? In what areas of my life have I insulted God with my worries and anxieties?

- *Peace.* How have I passively supported or actively promoted the violence that arises from apathy, prejudice, sexism, and discrimination? When and why have I refused to stand up and speak out for peace and justice? What has caused me distress and restlessness, and why have I continued to yield to it?

- *Patience.* In what areas of my life have I continued to support the false self's knee-jerk reaction to anger? When have I continued to fight against the things I cannot change or refused to accept the inconvenience that is part of daily life? Where have I given up on the desire and willingness to persevere, persist, and promote my relationships with God, others, and self?

- *Kindness.* How have I continued to focus upon myself, my wants, and my desires to the exclusion of others? What has hindered me from being compassionate, helpful, generous, and caring? Who have I continued to treat cruelly, heartlessly, and mercilessly, and why have I done this?

- *Generosity.* How have I continued to be a stingy and selfish person? When and why have I chosen to ignore the poor, the marginalized, and the needy? In what areas of my life have I continued to be self-absorbed, self-obsessed, and self-seeking?

- *Faithfulness.* How have I continued to betray a spouse, a relative, a friend, or a coworker? Where have I found myself slacking off in loyalty and dedication to public commitments? How have I allowed fear and anxiety to paralyze me and threaten me from living a life "full of faith"?

- *Gentleness.* What fear techniques have I used to ensure that I get my way? How have I pulled strings behind the scenes and manipulated situations to make sure that I remain in control? To whom and why have I been blunt, discourteous, brash, and brusque?

- *Self-control.* When have I freely given rein to hedonistic desires and fleeting desires? What tempting and sinful situations have I given myself permission to enter? Where in my life have self-mastery and interior freedom been overcome by bondage and slavery?

A commitment to some form of an examination of conscience is critical for anyone who is serious about the spiritual journey. Far from stirring up shame and guilt, its goal is the awareness of how our deliberate actions, habits, routines, and thoughts throw cold water on and even extinguish the fire of godly enthusiasm. Such an awareness can be brought to the Sacrament of Reconciliation, helps to free us from the false self, and facilitates the transformation by the Holy Spirit.

- PRACTICE

  Spend twenty minutes practicing an examination of conscience. The examination could be based upon the Pauline fruit found in Galatians or upon one of the other versions found on the Web.

  Spend time writing out this examination of conscience. Commit to sharing with your spiritual director the personal insights you discovered.

CHAPTER 28

THE CHALLENGE OF FORGIVENESS

∎

Gilbert went through an ugly divorce five years ago. Whenever he must talk to his ex-wife about their three children, his blood pressure goes up and he lashes out combatively. After those conversations, he finds himself stoking the fires of resentment and reliving the entire divorce. The pain continues even after five years. Gilbert has not forgiven his ex-wife and doubts if he ever will.

The simple truth is this: you can never be transformed into the image of Christ if you doggedly fuel a grudge and deliberately resist forgiving someone in your life.

The Decision

Jesus challenged the understanding of justice found in first-century Judaism. According to the Book of Exodus, justice was rendered by receiving an equitable compensation that balanced the scales of the wrong committed: "eye for eye, tooth for tooth" (21:24). Jesus, however, took exception to this. For him, there is only one form of just compensation, and it is *given* to the accused, not received by the accuser, because we ourselves have already been granted it by God: forgiveness. As the letter to the Colossians succinctly sums it up: "Just as the Lord has forgiven you, so you also must forgive" (3:13).

This form of countercultural justice is a decision, an act of the will. It is also a direct call to die to the false self and its need to find some way to get a petty form of revenge, to feel right and justified. It is not dependent upon an apology; some people, such as the sinful woman who washed Jesus's feet with her tears, have never learned the social grace of directly saying "I'm sorry" and asking for forgiveness (see

Luke 7:36–50). And Christian forgiveness does not wait to find some emotional space where it feels good to offer it; Jesus himself forgave his persecutors in the very midst of his betrayal even as he hung upon the cross (see Luke 23:34). Forgiveness is the limitless *choice* not to pick the scab, not to become entangled in the grudge, not to stoke the fires of anger and resentment by hugging the hurt or announcing it to others (see Matthew 18:22).

We often hug the hurt and pick the scab because it makes us feel powerful and intellectually right. We fail to remember, however, that keeping a grudge alive takes a lot of emotional energy. The more we invest in the grudge, the more we are sapped of our emotional stamina. Bitterness, anger, and self-pity become our evening cocktails as we surrender our serenity and inner peace; they help to continue the betrayal or hurt that occurred weeks, months, or even years ago.

Ultimately, if we don't want to commit to forgiveness in imitation of Christ, then we might want to consider forgiving because it's the best thing we can do for *ourselves*! It sets us free and closes the door on the past. Consequently, as the Mayo Clinic's website reminds us, compared with people who harbor grudges, those who forgive have healthier relationships, greater spiritual and psychological well-being, less anxiety and stress, lower blood pressure, fewer symptoms of depression, and a lower risk of alcohol and substance abuse. No other decision in our lives has such ability and power.

A Grace of the Holy Spirit

Leila and Daniel Abdallah of Sydney, Australia, know well that forgiveness is not only a decision but also a gift of the Holy Spirit. Their lives were suddenly and tragically upended on February 1, 2020, when 31-year-old Samuel William Davidson, driving at three times the speed limit under the influence of alcohol and drugs, struck and killed three of their children on a Sydney sidewalk as they walked to buy ice cream. They lost not only three of their six children but also a niece. Three more children, including another daughter, were severely injured. It was one of the worst road tragedies Australia has seen in recent memory.

This Maronite Christian couple managed to forgive the driver. Leila told a reporter, "Forgiveness at that time, I believe, came from the Holy Spirit." She continued, "I've been practicing forgiveness all my life, on a daily basis: when you forgive your parents, your siblings, your friends, your spouse," she said. "These are all small acts of forgiveness, but overall, you have to start forgiving the little things in order to be able to forgive the big things."

For her husband, Daniel, forgiveness didn't come as easily. It took what he called "a God moment" that changed his perspective on death. He began to see each passing day as "a day closer to reuniting with [my children]. Each anniversary is a year closer to reuniting with them. Death has now become something beautiful; it is no longer something foreign to us."

Daniel later stated that had he not been led to forgiveness, he would have "obsessed with the driver and his family, and on getting back at them. You have to find a greater good, that is a reason for forgiving. In our case, obedience to our Heavenly Father, and our three remaining children."

Leila added, "You don't have to be a nun to be a saint. You can find hope in tragedy, embrace pain, and forgive unconditionally. Always forgive unconditionally."

Noting that 65 percent of marriages end after the death of a child, Leila offers an additional grace of forgiveness. "Forgiveness is the key to a long-lasting relationship, and it has brought our marriage closer, helping us look forward to the future."[28]

The Abdallahs created the i4give Day and a website (www.i4give. com) to remember the four slain children. The annual remembrance is recognized by the government of Australia as a day to encourage all citizens to think about how forgiveness applies in their lives.

The Mechanics of Forgiveness

How do we come to make the decision to forgive? How do we facilitate this gift of the Holy Spirit? A wise spiritual director offered me some practical prompts.

I was hurt and angry when I was fired at the age of fifty-four. It was the first time I had ever experienced such a thing. Though the newly hired boss of the spiritual direction center used the polite language of "letting you go for financial reasons," I knew she was firing me because of my challenges to her competence as a professional and to the new direction she was giving to the center. Though I told the boss I would pack up and be out of my office within two weeks, I was actually gone within forty-eight hours. I still remember walking out of the office for the last time and muttering under my breath, "Good riddance."

Over the days that followed, I was obsessed with telling anyone who would listen about what had happened. And with each retelling, I would seethe and stoke the fire of resentment.

Within one month, I became more and more uncomfortable sitting so close to the campfire of anger. I knew I needed to move on, and that would only happen with forgiveness.

Familiar with the expression "Forgive and forget," I thought my future included erasing the incident from my memory. That proved impossible—and a violation of my self-respect. I was surprised when my spiritual director reminded me that forgiveness begins with remembering, not forgetting. I had to walk through the memory of the hurt and relive the event. I had to honestly admit to myself the emotional effects and personal consequences of this perceived betrayal. Without my doing that, forgiveness indeed would be a violation of myself.

My spiritual director then suggested that I take the challenging and empathic step of compassion: "Put yourself in the shoes of the boss and be as objective as you can." Why did she fire me? Did she intend to hurt me or was I overreacting? How did my actions and attitude contribute to the event? Was something else going on in her professional or personal life? As I tried to be as objective as possible and reflected upon these questions, I realized that as the new boss, Martha was trying to prove herself professionally and had the right to choose her own staff and run the center in the way she deemed fit. I also recognized how my brusque actions and judgmental attitude contributed to my firing. This step of compassion, as my spiritual director said, is a vivid reminder that words and actions sometimes say more about the offender than they say about the offended; and sometimes they speak volumes about the offended. Both were true in my case.

You have heard that it was said, "You shall love your neighbor and hate your enemy." But I say to you, Love your enemies and pray for those who persecute you, so that you may be children of your Father in heaven; for he makes his sun rise on the evil and on the good, and sends rain on the righteous and on the unrighteous. For if you love those who love you, what reward do you have? Do not even the tax collectors do the same?

Matthew 5:43–46

Forgiveness in no way condones the hurtful or offending action. That's why it is sometimes necessary—especially in cases of verbal or physical abuse—to develop self-protection strategies so we are not in harm's way again. Having said that, we must never allow these strategies to completely shut out the betrayer from our hearts. It takes some finesse to develop self-protection strategies and still be faithful to Jesus's challenge to love the enemy.

I previously made the point that forgiveness is a decision. And that decision is the heart and soul of the mechanics of forgiveness. We choose to offer forgiveness as a selfless gift with no strings attached. And in the case of the deepest wounds and most flagrant of betrayals, we typically have to commit to giving this gift again and again, even daily—and especially when we are tempted to take it back.

Six months after being fired, I ran into a former colleague of mine from the spiritual direction center. When he referred to my absence at the center, I was tempted to rehash my experience of being fired. But I reminded myself that I had forgiven Martha and had moved on. I remember saying to myself again, I have forgiven her and I am choosing to leave the past in the past.

The daily recommitment to this gift-giving shows the stuff of our soul and the intention of our heart. Even though the gift might simply lie in our heads as it did initially in my case, over time we will find it gradually making its way down to our hearts, where it loosens resentment and frees us from the past.

If, for whatever reason, we cannot offer forgiveness, it's helpful to ask, "What am I gaining by stoking the fire of resentment?" An honest answer typically reveals some kind of kickback that satisfies the false self. Perhaps it is the self-righteous need to feel justified and vindicated; perhaps it is some emotional issue from childhood that continues to play itself out. As we pray and reflect upon that question, we might gain further insight if we talk about the issues with a counselor or spiritual director. That helped me. Realize too that no one has ever arrived at the end of life and said, "I'm glad to have stayed angry and bitter for so long."

It's important to acknowledge that forgiveness does not always lead to reconciliation with the other person. Reconciliation takes the deliberate decision of both parties. And sometimes the other person is unwilling. It's a sad paradox that pardon and forgiveness sometimes are aching reminders of lost treasured relationships.

Forgiving Ourselves

Sometimes we are challenged to forgive ourselves. We look back at our lives and are filled with guilt and regret over something we did or didn't do some five years ago, five weeks ago, five days ago, or five minutes ago. Those feelings of guilt and regret often dampen the fire of our godly enthusiasm. They can sometimes even lead to self-loathing. Is there anything we can do to rekindle the fire of godly enthusiasm in our lives when we find ourselves sulking in remorse? I've found four actions helpful.

First, some of the guilt and shame can be alleviated by mentioning the event and the regret to a trusted friend, a spiritual director, a confessor, or a family member. I've been amazed in my life by the number of people who have shared similar events and feelings that my conscience has simmered and stewed over. Just knowing that I am not the only person on earth who has betrayed a friend, broken off communication with a family member, or passively displayed my anger by deliberately absenting myself from an important meeting, helps to dissipate some of my shame. As twelve-step programs remind us, "You're only as sick as your secrets." Spilling the beans and letting the cat out of the bag are important first steps in being set free from the past. In telling someone, I've also received some insightful advice that has helped me to understand my behavior and consequently, not repeat the regretful action.

Second, after exposing the action to another, it's wise not to dwell on the past. Mentally returning to the scene of the crime can only deepen your remorse and self-loathing. Feeding one's appetite with regretful, regurgitated memories of a past sin is neither helpful nor healthy. There's time-tested wisdom in the adage, "Leave the past in the past."

Third, have you ever asked yourself, "Was that really *me* who did *that*? Who *was* that person? How could *I* ever have done that?" Those questions betray a wise insight: transformative grace has been at work in your life! When you look at the past and can no longer recognize yourself as that sinner, there is cause for celebration. Without being aware of it, you have been catching fire by the grace of God's spark.

Fourth, be thankful and never forget the selfless acts of charity and compassion you have done because of God's grace. Those actions speak volumes about the true nature of your character and reveal it to be better than the worst of your sins.

The Spirit tries to mold our hearts according to the pattern of Jesus's forgiving, merciful, and compassionate heart. We can facilitate this transformation by remembering past hurts, empathizing with our betrayer, choosing to forgive, and recommitting daily to that decision. And that decision sometimes includes forgiving ourselves. Those choices break the stranglehold of the past and give us the freedom to enjoy life in the present.

■ PRACTICE

Find a place that offers the luxury of time and solitude; it could be in your home, at a park, or in a church. Once settled in a comfortable position, ask yourself, "Whom do I need to forgive? Why?" Once you have identified a person (and don't forget, it could be yourself), begin the decision to forgive by walking through the steps:

- Recall the incidents of betrayal or hurt.
- Put yourself in the other person's shoes and try to empathize with their hurtful word or action. When forgiving yourself, it's helpful to ask, "What was going on in my life that caused me to commit that sin?"
- Make the decision to forgive the person or yourself.
- Recommit to that decision every day until your heart softens and you are set free from the grudge or the remorse.

CHAPTER 29

INNER HEALING

■

In the previous chapter, I discussed the challenge of forgiveness—forgiving others and forgiving ourselves. Sometimes an emotional wound or trauma blocks us from making the decision to forgive and receiving the Spirit's gift of forgiveness. That wound or trauma forms a narrative for our lives. That narrative gives rise to an inner monologue: "I'm not talented." "I'm a terrible person." "I'm not lovable." "I'm a failure." Just like many people in the Gospels, we need to change, reframe, or rewrite the inner monologue of our lives to be open to the Spirit's transformation. That change can occur through inner healing.

The Ministry of Jesus

In his ministry, Jesus offered people the opportunity to break from the past and begin a new narrative for their lives. Matthew the tax collector left his post and became a disciple at the invitation of Jesus (see Matthew 9:9). Zacchaeus was called out of the sycamore tree and voluntarily offered to repent of his past fraud (see Luke 19:1–10). The woman caught in adultery was invited to break from her past and write a new narrative for her life with these simple words, "Go your way, and from now on do not sin again" (John 8:11).

And it wasn't just sinners who were invited to break from their past and write a new narrative for themselves. So were "the sick, those who were afflicted with various diseases and pains, demoniacs, epileptics, and paralytics" (Matthew 4:24). A leper was cleansed (see Matthew 8:1–4). Two blind men were healed (see Matthew 9:27–31). A paralytic was told, "I say to you, stand up, take your mat and go to your home" (Mark 2:11). The faith of a woman who suffered from hemorrhages for twelve years was acknowledged: "Daughter, your faith has made you well; go in peace, and be healed of your disease" (Mark 5:34). In Nain, a widow's son was restored to life (see Luke 7:11–17). Lazarus was raised from the dead (see John 11:1–44).

Besides sinners and the sick, those possessed by demons were set free from their past (see Matthew 9:32–34; Mark 1:21–28, 7:24–30, 9:14–29; Luke 9:37–43). Mark's narration of the healing of a demoniac in the Gentile country of the Gerasenes highlights in a vivid way how dark forces can imprison and isolate a person. The possessed man presented himself naked, living among the dead, unable to be restrained with shackles and chains, and sometimes "howling and bruising himself with stones" (Mark 5:5). Indeed, he appears subhuman, overcome with self-hatred. After Jesus released the legion of demons and sent them into swine, the man was found by the villagers "clothed and in his right mind" (v. 15). He wanted to go with Jesus, but Jesus refused him. "Go home to your friends, and tell them how much the Lord has done for you, and what mercy he has shown you" (v. 19). Freedom from demons led to freedom for mission.

The Power of the Past

Jesus's ministry to sinners, the sick, and demoniacs reminds us how easy it is to be imprisoned by our past. To break from the past and begin a new narrative sometimes require a healing of our memories. By revisiting a painful event and using a new interpretive lens, thus changing how we think and feel about the past, we give ourselves the ability to no longer be defined or disadvantaged by it. And with that healing, our hearts become eager kindling for the spark of God and the loving service of others.

Lack of love, the absence of a loving parent during one's formative years, the scars of sexual abuse, living in the shadow of a more talented sibling—these are wounds that never really heal. Just like the wounds still visible on the Risen Christ, some have so shaped our present identity that they remain with us forever. Yet, also like the wounds of the Risen Christ, these wounds *do stop bleeding*. They no longer drain us of our emotional and psychological energies. They no longer condemn us to our past and hinder our spiritual transformation. By the grace of God, they become our marks of victory and the very signs of God's healing power in our lives. They become proclamations that "death has been swallowed up in victory" (1 Corinthians 15:54). "For if we have been united with [Christ] in a death like his, we will certainly be united with him in a resurrection like his" (Romans 6:5).

These wounds stop bleeding and are transformed into the marks of resurrection the moment the desire for revenge is converted into the balm of mercy and forgiveness. That change—or emotional shift—or rewriting the narrative—often occurs through the grace of an insight. Sometimes a person arrives at that insight through some form of inner healing: psychotherapy, prayer, membership in twelve-step support groups, dialogue with a loved one or a trusted friend. I often suggest to my spiritual directees that they develop their own personal method of inner healing based upon five important principles. You'll quickly discover that these five principles closely resemble and even overlap with the dynamics involved in the challenge of forgiveness.

[God] heals the brokenhearted, and binds up their wounds.

Psalm 147:3

The Five Principles of Inner Healing

1. The continuing presence of a loving, compassionate Christ

The first principle of inner healing is that it is always done in the presence of Jesus the Divine Physician. He is the one who heals, comforts, and consoles. The Jesus who wept at the news of Lazarus's death is the same compassionate Jesus who ministers to us. He has an investment in our broken hearts. "The LORD is near to the brokenhearted and saves the crushed in spirit" (Psalm 34:18). One way of practicing this principle is to begin with the following prayer to Jesus the Healer:

Lord Jesus, you minister to the afflicted, abused, and abandoned. You are the healer of wounded and troubled hearts. I beg you to come into my life and heal me of the psychological harms and torments of my childhood that hinder my spiritual transformation. Heal the pain of my memories so I might be set free from the terrors of the night and be ablaze with godly enthusiasm.

O Lord, heal all those wounds that hinder me from being transformed into the image of Christ. Grant me the grace to forgive the people who inflicted those wounds—my parents, siblings, relatives, and friends. Apply the balm of your grace on the inner sores that continue to ooze with anger, rancor, and bitterness. Help me to live with the awareness that it costs too much to hang on to these hurts and keep fueling a grudge.

In my brokenness and weakness, I have injured others. Heal them before you heal me. May they one day come to forgive me.

Lord Jesus, you know my burdens through and through. I put them in your hands. Grant me the grace never to insult you by taking them back.

Heal, my Lord Jesus, those wounds that cause me physical illness and make me feel unwanted, unclean, and untouchable—

like the woman with a hemorrhage. I cry out for your compassion and your mercy. Let me touch the hem of your garment.

Above all, Lord Jesus, grant me the peace and joy that come from knowing you are the resurrection and the life. May the healing I pray for make me an authentic witness to your resurrection, your victory over sin and death, your living and healing presence among us. Amen.[30]

2. A review of the past event

As with forgiveness, we must go back to the past event and take another look at it. This is the hardest task of inner healing because we tend to live "around" our wounds, evading our hurts, skirting our scars. We rarely, if ever, confront them head on.

Mary has a fine reputation at the office. In public, she appears organized, upbeat, and fun loving. But her family and close friends see a different side of Mary: troubled, lethargic, drinking too much, constantly drained. Mary has spent most of her life refusing to confront some deep emotional issues that are probably centered on her mother whom she never refers to in conversation. Mary is living her life "around" her wound.

Our external behaviors often betray the fact that we are running away from something or actively repressing something. Sex, alcohol, workaholic busyness, uncontrollable anger—these are usually not the real problems. They are what we are doing *about* the problems. Think of them as aspirins we take to mask the pain of a headache.

The process of inner healing is avoiding the aspirins and confronting the headache. We come to grips with the present heartache caused by the past.

Many will argue that "returning to the scene of the crime" and "dragging up the past" are fruitless and waste time on things best forgotten. But we must remember that emotional wounds are like physical wounds: They do not heal if they are neglected. They remain and sometimes become infected.

This does not mean, however, that all wounds can—or should—be confronted *now*. We must not violate ourselves and force ourselves to grapple with issues or events that we are not ready to face. To do so can be dangerous.

Healing is not an achievement; it is a gift. When the time is right, the memory will "perk up" to the surface. That is a sign: it is time to begin the healing process. Until then, God has given us our defense mechanisms precisely to protect ourselves from the very issues or wounds that we are not yet ready to confront. Joan's tragedy offers a vivid example.

At an early age, Joan had been sexually abused by her uncle. For twenty-six years, she had repressed the memory of that abuse. At age thirty, she fell in love with Bill. At times she began to feel uncomfortable during their relationship but didn't quite understand why. She often projected those uncomfortable feelings upon Bill, blaming him for them. These mixed signals strained their relationship. Then dreams began, and Joan would awaken to feelings of stress and anxiety. Finally came conscious flashbacks to the past incident with her uncle. The wound was perking up. It was calling for attention and healing. It was time to face the past abuse.

Healing begins with the journey through the memory to the past—but in the presence of the Risen Christ. We must allow ourselves to enter again into the darkness of the betrayal, the abuse, the hurt, the wound. We expose the entire incident to the light shining through the wounds of the Risen Christ. We recall the details of the experience and the feelings it raised inside of us. At this point, as in the process of forgiving ourselves, verbalizing the experience to a caring friend or someone in the helping professions can be of utmost value.

3. The step of compassion

The third principle of inner healing is the challenge to step through our pain, anger, and hurt to place our feet in the shoes of the betrayer, to understand the heart of the betrayer. Think of the prodigal son parable, where the father encouraged his elder son to break through his resentment: "We had to celebrate and rejoice, because this brother of yours was dead and has come to life; he was lost and has been found" (Luke 15:32). Understanding breeds the gift of forgiveness, an important sign of inner healing.

Several questions help in that process of understanding our betrayer. Out of what emotional wound was the betrayer living? What pain filled the heart of the betrayer that would cause a person to react to us or treat us the way the betrayer did? How emotionally healthy is the betrayer? An insight will sometimes plant itself within our minds as we try to understand the betrayer's heart, as we walk in the shoes of the one who betrayed us, as we enter the flames of the betrayer's hell. Only when we understand the weaknesses and imperfections of others can we forgive them with humility and compassion.

Joan met regularly with a counselor. After several sessions, she found relief from some of her trauma as she gradually realized her uncle's psychological sickness.

Inner healing begins when we realize that most of the time, most people were doing the best they could. Sadly, the people who shape our broken personalities are broken themselves. Does that brokenness exonerate them from the trauma or injury they inflicted on us? Does that absolve or vindicate adults who deliberately betray our trust? No. The step of compassion has but one single purpose: to walk in the shoes of the betrayer, to realize that crippled people cannot walk without a limp. And life being as it is, we are all limping.

4. Calling upon the healing ministry of Christ

After we have called upon the presence of the Risen Christ, lived through the experience again in his presence, and tried to understand the heart of the betrayer with compassion and empathy, we can then take the next step in the process of inner healing. We turn to Jesus and ask him to minister to us.

The Risen Christ is both the physician and the balm. We allow the healing light that shines through his glorified wounds to penetrate the deep recesses and caverns of our broken hearts. "Christ and the power of his resurrection" (Philippians 3:10) will often burn away the ego's need to crusade, to be vindicated, to be justified, to have revenge. And through Christ's healing touch, light appears where darkness once prevailed. Life comes forth as Christ calls down the wounds of our past, "Come out!" Transformation begins as a spark lands on kindling and catches fire.

Sometimes, even after life is restored and our hearts are aflame, there is work to be done. After raising Lazarus, Jesus said to those standing by, "Unbind him, and let him go" (John 11:44). In restoring life to those areas in our past that have so wounded us or become painful, self-fulfilling prophecies, Jesus often enlists the help of others to unbind us. Thus, inner healing is often aided and abetted by professional counseling, spiritual direction, and membership in support groups.

5. The proclamation of new life

Over time—like forgiveness, inner healing is a process that doesn't occur with the snap of a finger in one sitting—and through God's grace, the wounds of the past stop bleeding. They no longer drain us of our emotional energy. The infections of anger, bitterness, and self-pity gradually fade from our lives. Though we cannot help looking at the world through the wounds and hurts that have shaped us, we begin to realize that it is not nearly as hostile as we originally thought.

Emotions shift. A new narrative emerges. We begin to walk on equal ground with other broken people who are sometimes in need of our forgiveness *again*.

We also find ourselves reaching through our wound(s) to extend a helping hand of compassion to those suffering the same pain or hurt that we once endured: freedom from the past leads to freedom for mission. We are sent to lovingly respond to the unmet need or required duty of the present moment. As Joan volunteers once a week at a shelter for battered women, she is very much aware that her past suffering has not been in vain; it has transformed her into an instrument of healing for others. She knows only too well that the God of all consolation has consoled her so that she might console others with the very consolation she herself has received (see 2 Corinthians 1:3–4).

The final step of healing comes when we can announce and witness to our own new life as Jesus instructed the former Gerasene demoniac. When someone asks Joan, "Where is that bitter, distrusting woman who was sexually violated by the very uncle she so innocently trusted?" she is quick to paraphrase the words of the angels at the tomb on Easter morning, "Why do you look for the living one among the dead? She is not here. She has been raised from the dead" (see Luke 24:5–6).

We are never condemned to the past. Never. No narrative is ever written in stone. Not one. Though the past's tight grip might constrict or burden our hearts and make us feel cursed, our compassionate God continues to offer us freedom from the past through divine grace and the prayer of inner healing.

■ PRACTICE

Find a time and place that offer silence and solitude. Look over your life, especially your childhood, and try to tease out incidents and events that have given rise to narratives that dampen your godly enthusiasm. One practical way of doing this is to ask yourself, "Why do I feel so angry? Why am I so unlovable? Why do I feel unnoticed and pushed aside?"

Once you have named the emotion that continues to hinder your spiritual growth, search for the origin of it. Having discovered the incident or event that gave rise to the emotion, commit to practicing the five principles of inner healing. Remember that inner healing is a process that occurs over time.

How will you facilitate the gift of inner healing that God wants to give you? Should you seek out a counselor or support group to help rewrite this narrative that is blocking your spiritual transformation? If so, commit to that.

Once freed from your past, how will you be sent on mission to others?

CHAPTER 30

RESISTING TEMPTATIONS

■

There are other serious and intentional commitments we must make if we want to be open to the Spirit's transformation. During this process, we quickly experience temptations by the devil that try to steer us away. We don't hear much about these temptations nowadays—but it is quite advantageous to discuss them. This is an essential topic for everyone who is serious about catching fire and becoming flame.

The Eight Tempting Thoughts

These temptations were enumerated by the fourth-century Christians who lived in the deserts of Egypt and Palestine. The desert fathers and mothers pinpointed eight thoughts that the devil uses to coax Christians into committing the seven deadly sins. They are thoughts toward pride, greed, anger, lust, gluttony, listlessness, vainglory, and dejection.

These thoughts fuel the four ego-obsessions of the false self: self-concern, self-image, self-gratification, and self-preservation. The desert monks discovered that entertaining these thoughts or giving them serious consideration weakens our resolve to resist them. That's why the monks thought it imperative to be aware of the insidious nature of these temptations and to learn how to confront them immediately.

To resist the devil's tempting thoughts, the desert fathers and mothers employed a technique called "talking back," reciting and repeating memorized Scripture as a method of defense. This technique would "cut off," to use the expression of the desert monks, the corresponding temptation.

Jesus's confrontation with the devil in the desert offered the early monks a valuable example in talking back to the devil's suggestions (see Matthew 4:1–11; Luke 4:1–13). In the initial temptation toward gluttony, Jesus was asked to change a stone into bread, thus suggesting a preoccupation with self-preservation. He instantly snapped back with a verse from the book of Deuteronomy. The second temptation concerned pride and self-gratification as the devil told Jesus he could presume angelic support in a precarious situation. Jesus retorted with another Scripture passage. Finally, the devil employed a temptation toward power and self-image, offering Jesus the kingdoms of the world if he would only worship him. Once again, Jesus talked back with a third verse, again from Deuteronomy.

The lesson offered to the desert monks and to us is obvious: don't fiddle and fuss with any tempting thought, trying to justify or rationalize what it might be asking of us; when we do, the slow dance of temptation begins as the devil wraps his claws around our minds and hearts and nudges us to commit the sins of pride, greed, anger,

Then the devil took him to Jerusalem, and placed him on the pinnacle of the temple, saying to him, "If you are the Son of God, throw yourself down from here, for it is written, 'He will command his angels concerning you, to protect you,' and 'On their hands they will bear you up, so that you will not dash your foot against a stone.'" Jesus answered him, "It is said, 'Do not put the Lord your God to the test.'" When the devil had finished every test, he departed from him until an opportune time.

Luke 4:9–13

lust, gluttony, acedia, or envy. Instead, we cut off the temptation by confronting it head on, naming it for what it is, and retorting with the truth proclaimed in Scripture. Such an immediate response keeps us focused on our call to be transformed into the image of Christ.

Here's a random selection of Scripture quotes that the desert monks recommended and used in talking back to the devil's tempting thoughts:

Pride

Do not say to yourself, "My power and the might of my own hand have gotten me this wealth." But remember the LORD *your God, for it is he who gives you power to get wealth, so that he may confirm his covenant that he swore to your ancestors, as he is doing today.* (Deuteronomy 8:17–18)

Toward the scorners he is scornful, but to the humble he shows favor. (Proverbs 3:34)

Why do you see the speck in your neighbor's eye, but do not notice the log in your own eye? (Matthew 7:3)

For all who exalt themselves will be humbled, and those who humble themselves will be exalted. (Luke 14:11)

But by the grace of God I am what I am, and his grace toward me has not been in vain. On the contrary, I worked harder than any of them—though it was not I, but the grace of God that is within me. (1 Corinthians 15:10)

Greed

If any of your kin fall into difficulty and become dependent on you, you shall support them; they shall live with you as though resident aliens. (Leviticus 25:35)

Do not withhold good from those to whom it is due, when it is in your power to do it. Do not say to your neighbor, "Go, and come again, tomorrow I will give it"—when you have it with you. (Proverbs 3:27–28)

Do not store up for yourselves treasures on earth, where moth and rust consume and where thieves break in and steal. (Matthew 6:19)

Then Jesus looked around and said to his disciples, "How hard it will be for those who have wealth to enter the kingdom of God!" (Mark 10:23)

Keep your lives free from the love of money, and be content with what you have; for he has said, "I will never leave you or forsake you." (Hebrews 13:5)

Anger

Then he sent his brothers on their way, and as they were leaving he said to them, "Do not quarrel along the way." (Genesis 45:24)

Refrain from anger, and forsake wrath. Do not fret—it leads only to evil. (Psalm 37:8)

Whoever is slow to anger has great understanding, but one who has a hasty temper exalts folly. (Proverbs 14:29)

But I say to you that if you are angry with a brother or sister, you will be liable to judgment; and if you insult a brother or sister, you will be liable to the council; and if you say, "You fool," you will be liable to the hell of fire. (Matthew 5:22)

Be angry but do not sin; do not let the sun go down on your anger, and do not make room for the devil. (Ephesians 4:26–27)

Lust

You shall not covet your neighbor's house; you shall not covet your neighbor's wife, or male or female slave, or ox, or donkey, or anything that belongs to your neighbor. (Exodus 20:17)

Do not desire [another's wife's] beauty in your heart, and do not let her capture you with her eyelashes; for a prostitute's fee is only a loaf of bread, but the wife of another stalks a man's very life. (Proverbs 6:25–26)

But I say to you that everyone who looks at a woman with lust has already committed adultery with her in his heart. (Matthew 5:28)

Do not be deceived! Fornicators, idolaters, adulterers, male prostitutes, sodomites, thieves, the greedy, drunkards, revilers, robbers— none of these will inherit the kingdom of God. (1 Corinthians 6:9–10)

Be sure of this, that no fornicator or impure person, or one who is greedy (that is, an idolater), has any inheritance in the kingdom of Christ and of God. (Ephesians 5:5)

Gluttony

The LORD *does not let the righteous go hungry, but he thwarts the craving of the wicked.* (Proverbs 10:3)

Do not be among winebibbers, or among gluttonous eaters of meat; for the drunkard and the glutton will come to poverty, and drowsiness will clothe them with rags. (Proverbs 23:20–21)

Let us live honorably as in the day, not in reveling and drunkenness, not in debauchery and licentiousness, not in quarreling and jealousy. Instead, put on the Lord Jesus Christ, and make no provision for the flesh, to gratify its desires. (Romans 13:13–14)

Now, discipline always seems painful rather than pleasant at the time, but later it yields the peaceful fruit of righteousness to those who have been trained by it. (Hebrews 12:11)

Listlessness

Wait for the LORD, *and keep to his way, and he will exalt you to inherit the land; you will look on the destruction of the wicked.* (Psalm 37:34)

How long will you lie there, O lazybones? When will you rise from your sleep? A little sleep, a little slumber, a little folding of the hands to rest, and poverty will come upon you like a robber, and want, like an armed warrior. (Proverbs 6:9–11)

And everyone who has left houses or brothers or sisters or father or mother or children or fields, for my name's sake, will receive a hundredfold, and will inherit eternal life. (Matthew 19:29)

Rejoice in hope, be patient in suffering, persevere in prayer. (Romans 12:12)

For you need endurance, so that when you have done the will of God, you may receive what was promised. For yet "in a very little while, the one who is coming will come and will not delay; but my righteous one will live by faith. My soul takes no pleasure in anyone who shrinks back." (Hebrews 10:36–38)

Vainglory

Let another praise you, and not your own mouth—a stranger, and not your own lips. (Proverbs 27:2)

Beware of practicing your piety before others in order to be seen by them; for then you have no reward from your Father in heaven. (Matthew 6:1)

"Let the one who boasts, boast in the Lord." For it is not those who commend themselves that are approved, but those whom the Lord commends. (2 Corinthians 10:17–18)

Am I now seeking human approval, or God's approval? Or am I trying to please people? If I were still pleasing people, I would not be a servant of Christ. (Galatians 1:10)

Do not love the world or the things in the world. The love of the Father is not in those who love the world. (1 John 2:15)

Dejection

You are a hiding place for me; you preserve me from trouble; you surround me with glad cries of deliverance. (Psalm 32:7)

Do not rejoice over me, O my enemy; when I fall, I shall rise; when I sit in darkness, the LORD will be a light to me. (Micah 7:8)

Do not let your hearts be troubled. Believe in God, believe also in me. (John 14:1)

I consider that the sufferings of this present time are not worth comparing with the glory about to be revealed to us. (Romans 8:18)

For godly grief produces a repentance that leads to salvation and brings no regret, but worldly grief produces death. (2 Corinthians 7:10)

We are easily deceived and duped by temptation. That's why the desert Christians were quick to quote Jesus's hyperbolic teaching, "If your hand or your foot causes you to stumble, cut it off and throw it away; it is better for you to enter life maimed or lame than to have two hands or two feet and to be thrown into the eternal fire" (Matthew 18:8; see also Matthew 5:29–30; 18:9). We must remain single-hearted, not entertaining two masters (see Matthew 5:8; 6:24). "But strive first for the kingdom of God and his righteousness" (Matthew 6:33) is a clarion call to remain attentive and focused and to cut off any tempting thought as soon as it arises.

Other Strategies for Dealing with Temptations

How do we keep that attention and focus? By keeping vigilance over our thoughts and inner monologues. They are the devil's first line of seduction. As soon as we find ourselves justifying or rationalizing an action consistent with any of the eight tempting thoughts, we are not far from giving in to it. Simple awareness can be the beginning of cutting off temptation.

We also need to be vigilant over the heart's feelings and our cerebral reactions to situations. Feelings and emotions such as pride, lust, or anger are neither right nor wrong in themselves. They are neutral. They are typically the knee-jerk reactions of our heart. However, the way we entertain, express, or vent them will sometimes get us dancing with the devil and later committing sin.

We can so closely identify with a temptation that we begin to believe that we *are* the temptation and therefore cannot resist it. Our rationalization for giving in is simple: "This is just who I am." But we are all so much more than our superficial thoughts and the emotions they elicit from us.

Some temptations keep returning and discouraging or embarrassing us. The tempting thought of listlessness whispers, "Oh, you might as well give in, since you obviously haven't outgrown it." In this instance, it's important to remember that temptations will dissipate when we stand up and talk back to them. When they return, we talk back again. And again. And again. That's the very nature of temptations. They are desperate. They keep buzzing around until they find something on which to land.

I once co-preached a weekend retreat with a good friend. He offered us a keen insight: there is a dignity in doggedly standing up and stubbornly resisting temptation time and again. That persistence speaks volumes about the fire in our lives and our commitment to the Spirit's transformative process.

Knowing ourselves and our weaknesses goes a long way in pinpointing where we need to be vigilant. Temptations rarely occur where we are strong and confident; if they do, we quickly talk back to them and cut them off. For example, I am usually self-confident and feel secure about my life and the choices I have made. Consequently, I rarely am tempted toward envy; if I am, I quickly stand up to the tempting thought, and it immediately goes up in smoke. However, there are other areas in my life—in relationships and how I am so judgmental—where I am weak and stand on shaky ground. In these areas, I need to focus my attention, be vigilant, and pray for the strengthening grace of perseverance.

The desert fathers and mothers also remind us to be proactive in our struggles with temptations. Rather than simply waiting around until temptations arise and then talking back and resisting them, we are called to live the virtues that attack the very roots of the eight tempting thoughts. The proactive virtues (and the tempting thoughts they attack) are:

- charity (pride)
- generosity (greed)
- patience (anger)
- chastity (lust)
- self-control (gluttony)
- perseverance (listlessness)
- humility (vainglory)
- diligence (dejection)

These virtues aid the Spirit in the process of transformation.

Blazing with the fire of godly enthusiasm is no easy task. It requires not only trust in the Spirit of God but also an awareness of and resistance to myriad temptations that come our way each and every day. We do not do that alone. Keep in mind that we also can rely upon the help of the great High Priest who was tempted in every way possible but never sinned (see Hebrews 4:15).

■ PRACTICE

Reflect upon a situation when your defenses are typically down. What tempting thought arises? Rehearse in your mind how you will talk back to the temptation with one of the recommended Scripture passages. Also commit to intentionally practicing the appropriate proactive virtue that challenges that tempting thought.

CHAPTER 31

SURRENDER AND ABANDONMENT

∎

As you are discovering, spiritual transformation and becoming all flame require more than God's grace, kindling, and spiritual practices that help fan the spark of God. They also require intentional commitments—like the examination of conscience, forgiveness, inner healing, and resisting temptations—that are challenging and seemingly stretch us beyond our limits. And the commitments don't stop there.

Tony has multiple sclerosis and is in a wheelchair. I will never forget a conversation I had with him a few years ago.

"Father, I've been in this wheelchair now for more than fifteen years. I've begged God to heal me, to give me the grace to stand up, push this wheelchair away, and walk on my own. I've prayed and prayed and still get no reply. Why won't God answer my prayer?"

Using his right hand and hitting the right armrest of the wheelchair, he continued, his voice cracking with emotion, "This is the enemy. This is my chain of slavery."

"Tony," I said, tapping the right armrest, "this is not the enemy or a chain of slavery. This is your path to holiness. And the moment you can surrender and accept it is the moment you will be freed from it. Embrace it. Then you'll go on your way—*in* it."

The Cross in Our Lives

I know this lesson can be a difficult one to accept. We each have a cross that we have prayed to be delivered from or wish we could change. It could be a burden, worry, trial, tribulation, misfortune, hardship, misery, suffering, or sorrow; it might be cut and hewn in the form of a divorce, a friend's betrayal, the loss of a job, financial challenges, the diagnosis of a terminal illness, or the effects of a natural disaster. Whatever it is, we spend too much time and energy trying to walk away from it or refashion it in a way that is more acceptable to us.

Jesus himself experienced this human struggle as he faced his impending death. In the Garden of Gethsemane, he fell into a state of dreadful agony and prayed, "Father, if you are willing, remove this cup from me; yet, not my will but yours be done" (Luke 22:42). He struggled to live out his intention of abandonment. "In his anguish he prayed more earnestly, and his sweat became like great drops of blood falling down on the ground" (v. 44).

There is a clear emotional shift, however, evidenced in the way he peacefully submitted to being arrested (see verses 47–53), his refusal to offer a self-defense before the assembly of Jewish elders and Pilate (see vv. 66–71; 23:1–5), and his silence before Herod (see 23:9). Moreover, his final words from the cross boldly proclaim that his intention had become reality as he handed over his life to God: "Father, into your hands I commend my spirit" (23:46). In that final act of surrender and abandonment, Jesus lovingly offered one of his greatest gifts to his Father: faith and trust.

If any want to become my followers, let them deny themselves and take up their cross and follow me.

Matthew 16:24

Called to spiritual transformation, we must learn to accept the cross in our lives. Jesus makes this the prerequisite for every disciple. So important is this that the Gospel tradition repeats it five times (see Matthew 10:38; 16:24; Mark 8:34; Luke 9:23; 14:27). It's a paradox in the spiritual life: the wood of the cross is indispensable kindling for the fire of godly enthusiasm.

The Act of Abandonment

I gradually became used to the Chinese culture and acclimatized to its living conditions. My previous struggles with adjustment had dissipated. I was confident with my language skills, had many local friends, and a job as director of human resources for a large, international accounting firm that provided a resident/working visa to keep me legal while I ministered on weekends as the pastor to Roman Catholics. I had settled in and just assumed I would spend the rest of my life as a "newfangled" missionary among the Chinese people.

One Sunday afternoon as I left my apartment to attend a meeting of parishioners, I noticed a marked "Security Police" automobile parked outside. The apartment's receptionist commented that two men had been inquiring about me, my activities, and my employment. As I got into a taxi to go to my meeting, the police started their car and followed me. It quickly became apparent that my cover had been blown and the Chinese government knew who I was, where I lived, and what I was doing. Realizing that my time as a missionary to the Chinese would have to come to an end, I got a lump in my throat. Over the following weeks, I became depressed as I struggled to understand why God had brought me to the other side of the world only to have this happen after almost twelve years. During a phone conversation, a wise priest advised me, "Don't try and figure it out. Just accept it and trust that God has another adventure in store for you." It took me more than two months before I begrudgingly resigned myself to his advice.

Surrender and acceptance of the cross—be it a disappointment, misfortune, or sorrow—require an act of abandonment. One of the most difficult spiritual commitments, it demands that we put our faith and trust into action. It is a far cry from my own passive act of begrudging resignation, offered with a defenseless and defeated sigh, characterized by regret that smolders among the ashes.

The abandonment to God's will by Christian disciples is characterized by the trust known to mature believers. Think in terms of the fire of a lover's selflessness. Those who have been enflamed by that selflessness and trust willingly let go of the false self's wishes and its egotistical obsessions. They joyfully receive and respond to the unmet need or required duty of the present moment, however taxing, painful, or inconvenient. They peacefully submit to whatever way the Spirit chooses to continue the transformative process of the spiritual life. This is the abandonment that shaped the life of Jesus— and should shape the lives of his disciples.

This abandonment requires what the spiritual tradition calls holy indifference. The English word *indifference* is unfortunate, because it implies living with careless apathy, irresponsible disinterest, or a hardened lack of concern. Holy indifference, however, means living from a place of interior freedom where my heart is no longer constricted by egotistical demands but burns with a loving faith crackling with trust in God. It is captured in the phrase of the traditional wedding vows, "for better, for worse, for richer, for poorer, in sickness and in health." I am open and accept each and every situation.

Floating in water provides a useful analogy. The more we struggle to float in a swimming pool—and consequently maintain control—the more we will fail and sink to the bottom. Floating requires that we let go and give ourselves over to the water. It requires a kind of trust in the buoyancy of water.

The same is true with the abandonment born of holy indifference; it requires trust and is not about resignation. As when we let go and give ourselves over to the water, we surrender ourselves and willingly submit to the mystery of life that God sets before us—"for better, for worse, for richer, for poorer, in sickness and in health." That includes actively yielding to things we are powerless to change, knowing that God is ever-present and trusting that the Spirit is at work. We deliberately pick up that cross. We embrace it. And in our acceptance, surrender, and embrace, the God who yearns to be in a relationship with us sparks us into people of godly enthusiasm who will know the power of the Resurrection.

Saint Charles de Foucauld, canonized by Pope Francis in 2022, surrendered to the cross as a martyr in Algeria, North Africa, in 1916. He wrote a prayer that captures the spirit of abandonment that Jesus himself had and that we are all called to have. This is the prayer offered by the surrendered, accepting heart:

> Father,
> I abandon myself into your hands.
> Do with me what you will.
> Whatever you may do, I thank you. I am ready for all, I accept all.
> Let only your will be done in me and in all your creatures.
> I wish no more than this, O Lord. Into your hands I commend
> my soul.
> I offer it to you with all the love of my heart,
> for I love you, Lord, and so need to give myself, to surrender
> myself into your hands without reserve and with boundless
> confidence, for you are my Father.[31]

■ PRACTICE

Commit to slowly and meditatively praying Saint Charles de Foucauld's prayer of abandonment for an entire week—then memorizing it. When you find yourself fighting against the cross in your life, pray it as a way to strengthen your own surrender and abandonment.

CHAPTER 32

REVEAL EVERYTHING TO GOD

■

Spiritual transformation is about growing in intimacy with God. And intimacy requires vulnerability and openness—the kind of vulnerability and openness you show when you reveal *everything* to your beloved. This is a commitment to total and complete honesty.

Many Christians find that keeping a spiritual journal helps to foster that commitment. Unlike a regular journal that typically records the *facts* of our lives (who, what, when, where, why, how), a spiritual journal records our *feelings* (joy, sadness, fear, disappointment, peacefulness, anger, discouragement, frustration, etc.), *impressions* ("this could possibly mean that . . ."), *hunches* ("my gut tells me . . ."), and *responses* ("my immediate reaction was . . .") to the facts of our lives, especially about the process of being transformed by the Spirit of God. In a spiritual journal, we have a heart-to-heart conversation, conveying the contours of the soul in script.

As you sit down to write in your spiritual journal, consciously choose not to be distracted by the cellphone, the doorbell, or the timer on the oven. This is sacred time that deserves your respect and reverence. As in or with other moments and movements of grace, give yourself over to the process; surrender to any amount of time the process might ask of you. You don't want to be rushed as you reflect and write.

Start in silence. Closing your eyes, breathing deeply, and sipping some coffee or tea are great ways to settle down and become attentive as you pause, ponder and pray over your life. You might want to say a prayer to the Holy Spirit before starting to explore this moment or event in the history of your own transformation.

It's best to date each entry. This can be helpful in the future when you want to retrieve your feelings and reactions to different experiences. It also provides a historical context for your spiritual growth and awareness.

Write honestly and naturally—whether that be quickly or deliberately, not allowing the inner critic to edit or delete anything considered inappropriate. You don't have to write eloquently or even in complete sentences; after all, you're writing for yourself and not for an audience. This openness, vulnerability, and honesty breed divine revelation and self-revelation; they are the building blocks of intimacy.

When journaling, I begin by answering the questions used in preparation for a spiritual direction appointment:

> Your very lives are a letter that anyone can read by just looking at you. Christ himself wrote it—not with ink, but with God's living Spirit; not chiseled into stone, but carved into human lives— and we publish it.
>
> 2 Corinthians 3:3, MSG

- What is the most important thing going on in my life right now, and how do I feel about it?
- What is God doing in my life right now?
- Where and how is the Spirit nudging me?
- How am I responding to God's call in my daily life?
- What am I deliberately fighting against or resisting?

Your journal doesn't have to consist only of sentences. As they say, a picture is worth a thousand words. Sometimes a doodle, photograph, or newspaper advertisement says it best! Or a metaphor or simile might spontaneously come to mind that captures exactly where you are: "I feel as if the sun is setting, and I am sinking in quicksand." Perhaps we have seen something in nature that triggers a memory, a feeling, or an insight: "I saw that bird feed her chicks and instantly thought how God has been nursing me in the past few weeks."

When I first started journaling, I used to get discouraged, thinking I had to write in my journal every day. Nothing could be further from the truth. Some seasons in life call me to write daily; others call me to write weekly or monthly. It's important to personally discover the frequency and rhythm that work best.

Each of the four annual seasons provides an opportune time for Bradley, one of my spiritual directees, to review his past journal entries. Sometimes, in looking over what he has written over a particular season, he discovers in hindsight an important thread of God's grace weaving together the story of his life. Sometimes it is in reading past entries that he experiences God's revelation—"Oh, now I get it," he says to himself—or comes to a deeper awareness of himself and how he is responding to the action of God's Spirit. Some people follow Bradley's practice of reading past entries when an opportunity arises. Other people, like Sherry, don't find it helpful to read past entries; for them, the instant revelation that sometimes comes during the process of writing is helpful enough. You'll soon discover what's useful for you.

Other Journal Entries

A spiritual journal can also include "ah-ha" moments of divine revelation: new insights into Scripture, biblical prayers that we find meaningful, and passages from spiritual books that are worth highlighting and remembering. It can also document our sins, hurts, limitations, longings, discernment processes, insights, and deepest desires.

In the back of my own spiritual journal, as I read past entries, I keep a running list titled "What Life Has Taught Me about God and Myself." I record the date and state the insight or realization, followed in parentheses by the event in my life to which it refers. Here's an example:

September 17, 1980. God is my father who will never abandon me (Dad's suicide and the financial consequences that followed it in 1968).

Here's another example:

November 8, 2011. Gratitude keeps me aware that my talents are gifts freely given by God. Talents are not my property, and I am not a "self-made" man (the invitation from a publisher to write a book for them).

Here's an insight from praying with Scripture that I recorded in that list and that has shaped my personal spirituality:

January 4, 2016. God is the divine widow and I'm the judge. Each and every day, God comes into my life and asks of me something that only I can do for the sake of the kingdom. So I must listen to my life because God uses the people I encounter, the situations I find myself in, my deepest feelings, and my most creative thoughts as the megaphone to convey his will for me (praying over the parable of the persistent widow found in Luke 18:1–5).

This ongoing list becomes a document of God's revelation and my own self-awareness.

A spiritual journal can also be "a sanctuary in script" where we go for intimate conversations with God and others. We might write a letter to God—or have God write a letter to us. We might write out a dialogue with a deceased relative, a person from Scripture, or even an individual from the history of Christian spirituality who has influenced us. Though this kind of writing might feel awkward or contrived at first, giving ourselves over to the process can provide the grace for gaining a deeper understanding of others, for healing old emotional wounds, and for providing closure to unresolved issues in past relationships.

The spiritual journal is meant to increase our sensitivity to the Spirit's transformative process and our commitment to being vulnerable, open, and honest with God. Any writing technique that helps to foster that sensitivity and intimacy is well worth trying. For many of us, the journal becomes our go-to place for pondering and treasuring the gifts, graces, and blessings bestowed upon the heart.

■ PRACTICE

Commit a few hours to reflecting upon your entire life: your earliest memories, your childhood, your adolescence, and the choices and decisions you have made in adulthood. Take your time with this process. Then begin to write out your own list entitled, "What Life Has Taught Me about God and Myself." What do these statements tell you about God's enthusiasm to be in a relationship with you, and about your response?

CHAPTER 33

SILENCE AND SOLITUDE: THE RETREAT

■

The intimacy required for spiritual transformation takes more than the vulnerability, openness, and honesty we bring to keeping a spiritual journal. It also requires an intentional commitment to spending time with a God whom "no one has ever seen" (see 1 John 4:12). Though there are many ways to do that—in prayer or loving service, for example—one of the most challenging ways is in the silence and solitude of a retreat.

I know people who feel threatened by the hush of silence and the loneliness of solitude. They maneuver themselves into real or virtual relationships and conversations or listen to podcasts or find some other way to run from the dreaded S&S. But authentic spiritual transformation does not allow us to escape the need for silence and solitude.

Silence compels us to unplug the noise in our lives, to close our mouths, and to confront the vast, arid expanse within us. The psalmist enjoins us, "Be still and know that I am God! I am exalted among the nations, I am exalted in the earth" (Psalm 46:10), or, as Eugene Peterson graphically paraphrases it, "Step out of the traffic! Take a long, loving look at me, your High God, above politics, above everything" (MSG). Unfortunately, most of us prefer the racket of the traffic to the stillness of silence.

Solitude challenges us to break away from family and friends and come to grips with the junk food stuffed in our lunch boxes and the clutter hoarded and stacked against the walls in our hearts. It is the place where, according to Henri Nouwen, we remove the "scaffolding"[32] of our lives: friends, telephone calls, meetings, music, and books. It's where, without all our props and diplomas, we stand naked before the living God and confront the reality of who we *really* are and not who we dress to be every day. "What you are before God, that you are and nothing more."[33] Far from a spiritual spa or therapeutic clinic, solitude is, as Nouwen rightly notes, "the furnace of transformation."[34]

The Desert of the Annual Retreat

Jesus, full of the Holy Spirit, returned from the Jordan and was led by the Spirit in the wilderness, where for forty days he was tempted by the devil. He ate nothing at all during those days, and when they were over, he was famished. . . . But now more than ever the word about Jesus spread abroad; many crowds would gather to hear him and to be cured of their diseases. But he would withdraw to deserted places and pray.

Luke 4:1–2; 5:15–16

According to the Gospels, immediately after Jesus's baptism, the Spirit led him into the solitude of the desert (see Matthew 4:1–11; Mark 1:12–13; Luke 4:1–13). This was like a training camp at which Jesus confronted his enemy. The circumstance and the weeks of prayer no doubt confirmed in him the purpose of his mission and the fiery passion for his Father's will. He emerged from the desert "proclaiming the good news of God and saying, 'The time is fulfilled, and the kingdom of God has come near; repent, and believe in the good news'" (Mark 1:14–15). After his desert time, Jesus was "filled with the power of the Spirit" (Luke 4:14) and would periodically retreat again into silence and solitude (see Luke 5:16; Mark 1:35).

Like many other people, I find an annual retreat to be an important time to intentionally follow Jesus into silence and solitude. In many respects, it is a deliberate extension of my daily prayer time. Leaving my cellphone and tablet behind, I temporarily retreat from my present surroundings, disengage from my relationships, and confront the fragility of my life. Suprisingly, this helps to reignite my passion and enthusiasm as I surrender to the Spirit's process of transforming me into the image of Christ.

Kinds of Retreats

Over the past forty-five years, I have discovered that a retreat can take on a variety of forms.

The *thirty-day Ignatian retreat* (often called the Spiritual Exercises) is done once, at most twice, in life and was designed by St. Ignatius of Loyola not only to help participants discover God's presence in their lives but also to help foster a personal commitment to becoming Christ's coworker for the kingdom. The person making the retreat goes to a retreat house for thirty consecutive days of prayer and reflection. The person spends four to six hours a day meditating upon selected Scriptures based on four successive themes and then meets every day with a director to share the fruits of the meditations.

For those like me unable to take off thirty consecutive days for solitude, Ignatius designed the *retreat in daily life* (called the Nineteenth Annotation). Offering the basic dynamic of the thirty-day retreat, it can take place at home during the course of daily routines and job responsibilities. Conducted over a period of several months to more than a year, it requires daily prayer and scriptural meditation. A retreatant typically meets once a week or every two weeks with a director to discuss his or her reflections on the Scriptures. This format offered me the opportunity to try out in real life what I was learning and discovering during this retreat. Creighton University offers a popular online version of this retreat at https://onlineministries.creighton.edu/CollaborativeMinistry/cmo -retreat.html

Preached weekend retreats usually begin on Thursday or Friday evening and last until Sunday noon. In an atmosphere of silence and solitude at a retreat house, a preacher will be invited to offer four to six thirty-minute talks on a specific theme, such as the Beatitudes, the Lord's Prayer, women in Scripture, the gifts of the Holy Spirit, or some other topic chosen by the preacher. Between these large-group sessions, retreatants spend time walking, meditating, journaling, reading, praying the Stations of the Cross, and perhaps celebrating the Sacrament of Reconciliation. Preached retreats are offered in most Catholic retreat houses across the United States.

Similar to preached retreats, *guided retreats* feature a preacher. In a guided retreat, there is usually only one extended conference or talk per day, lasting forty-five minutes to an hour. Afterward, those making the retreat spend the rest of the day in silence and solitude reflecting upon what they have heard. In the evening, there might be an optional group sharing or prayer service, based upon the theme of the day's conference.

Directed retreats are tailor-made, focused on an individual's specific needs. They can last anywhere from a weekend to a week. I make a weeklong directed retreat every two years and appreciate meeting with an assigned director every day during the retreat for twenty to thirty minutes. I discuss with the director some issue in my life that I am struggling with or discerning, or how I am or am not responding to the transformative grace of the Holy Spirit in my life. On occasion, the director has given me homework to do for the day, such as reading and meditating upon a passage of Scripture. Think of it as an intensive period of spiritual direction with an assigned director who listens to you with a pair of ears different from those of your usual spiritual director and offers his or her own thoughts, comments, and insights.

During the pandemic of 2020, many people found themselves stuck inside with too much time on their hands. So I began offering a hybrid of the directed retreat which I called a *virtual directed retreat* that I continue to offer. The retreatant agreed to spend thirty minutes every day in prayer, reflection, or spiritual reading. Some of my retreatants asked for a different Gospel passage every day to meditate and reflect upon. Others worked through one of my books or one of the great classics of Christian spirituality such as *Introduction to the Devout Life*, *Abandonment to Divine Providence*, or *The Practice of the Presence of God*. I committed to thirty-minute meetings with the retreatant for five consecutive days at the same time of day via Zoom.

The years I don't make a directed retreat, I make a *private retreat*. This is a self-designed retreat. I go to a retreat house or hermitage to be alone. I'm on my own as I plan my daily schedule, sometimes my meals, and how I will spend my time. Everyone does private retreats differently, but I typically spend part of every day in extended prayer, reading a book or praying with Scripture, reflecting upon the past year, and journaling. I also take a long walk. Of all the different kinds of retreats, the private retreat was the most intimidating for me initially since it comes the closest to providing the experience of the silence and solitude of Jesus in the desert.

No matter how they are packaged, the silence and solitude experienced in a retreat are important. By stripping us of our electronic devices and the distractions of other creature comforts, a retreat challenges us to recommit again to stoking the flame of godly enthusiasm in our lives.

■ PRACTICE

Go online to find a nearby retreat center. If you have trouble finding one, contact your local church for suggestions and recommendations. Get information about the retreat center's upcoming retreats and commit to making one within the next year. If you've never made a retreat before, it's wise not to bite off more than you can chew; choose a preached weekend retreat and start there. While on retreat, write about the experience in a journal. After the retreat, discuss your experience with your spiritual director.

CHAPTER 34

SABBATH REST

■

The transformation into a Christlike flame blazing in the world isn't accomplished simply by *doing* things in response to God's grace. Paradoxically, it also requires a dynamic commitment that gives us cause to pause—literally! Becoming all flame is as much about *being* as it is about *doing*.

A friend told me his life was "like being driven in an old, clunky automobile with a stuck gas pedal; it's going to stop by either running into something or running out of gas." That description fits so many of us: we are driven workaholics whose lives are potentially out of control and headed in a fatal direction.

In our work-obsessed world, the spiritual practice of taking a day off is countercultural. The Sabbath rest appears downright unnatural. The very word *Sabbath*, derived from the Hebrew for "stop, cease, desist, pause, rest," indicates that such rest requires a deliberate act of the will. For some of us, that will sound like fingernails scratching against the blackboard.

Scriptural Foundations

The religious origins of the weekly Sabbath, from Friday sundown to Saturday sundown, are rooted in the Jewish Scriptures. While wandering in the desert, the Israelites were told that the seventh day of the week was "a day of solemn rest, a holy sabbath to the Lord" (Exodus 16:23) when all work was forbidden (see Exodus 20:8–10; 31:13–17; Deuteronomy 5:12–14). Though the prohibitions against various kinds of work, such as lighting fires, cooking, and pressing grapes (see Exodus 16:23, 35:3; Nehemiah

13:15) strike twenty-first-century ears as overly detailed and maybe even picayune, the explicit point was that this day was meant to be a break in the action, an armistice from the daily grind and drudgery, a day of joyful and peaceful relaxation.

The Sabbath was sacred because it was a sign of the covenant made with Moses and his descendants on Mt. Sinai (see Exodus 31:13). It acknowledged God as the Creator of time and the universe and allowed the Israelites to experience the rest that God himself had experienced (Exodus 31:17; see also 20:11). It also reminded the chosen people of their former slavery in Egypt and the wonderful Exodus wrought by God on their behalf (Deuteronomy 5:15). And so the Sabbath was a weekly reminder to the Israelites of who God is and what God did to satisfy his fiery passion to be in a relationship with them.

By the time of Jesus, the Sabbath rest as interpreted by the scribes and Pharisees had become a legalistic yoke and burden. With stunning insight, Jesus retrieved its original intention. It once again became a restful and leisurely celebration of God's enthusiasm for the chosen people.

The Sabbath was made for humankind, and not humankind for the Sabbath.

Mark 2:27

Though a former strict observer of the Jewish law, Paul did not consider the Sabbath as obligatory for Christians (see Colossians 2:16; Galatians 4:9–10; Romans 14:5), especially as Christianity attracted more and more Gentiles and the Jewish Christian churches disappeared. Sunday quickly replaced Saturday and became the Lord's Day, when Christians gathered and broke bread together in the Eucharist (see Acts 20:7; 1 Corinthians 16:2). The first day of the week was chosen, it being the day of Christ's resurrection; it represented new life and a new creation.

Rest as Sacred Time

In our compulsive, work-driven culture, observing Sabbath rest is perceived to be wasting time that could be better served in productivity. So why do we get off the driven treadmill of routine? Because there is something holy and Godlike about deliberately choosing to give ourselves a break and entering into the Creator's experience of resting and being refreshed. A famous shoe commercial used to push us to lace up our shoes and "Just do it." Similarly, the practice of Sabbath rest challenges us to remove our shoes as Moses did before the burning bush, prop up our feet, and just be. Like God on the seventh day of creation, we look back on the fruits of our week's labors and we enjoy them. We gather up the loose and frazzled corners of our lives and for this sacred time bring them together as a way of honoring who we are before God. Sabbath rest is about refreshment, reflection, and recollection.

As the Jewish theologian Abraham Joshua Heschel insightfully writes in *The Sabbath: Its Meaning for Modern Man*, "It must always be remembered that the Sabbath is not an occasion for diversion or frivolity; not a day to shoot fireworks or to turn somersaults, but an opportunity to mend our tattered lives; to collect rather than to dissipate time."[35]

There are myriad ways to take advantage of this "opportunity," as Heschel calls it. They include the following:

- Celebrate the Eucharist in your parish and offer the fruits of your week's labors along with the bread and wine.
- Take a walk in the park or in a nearby arboretum and experience the fruits of God's labors found in creation.
- Spend some quality time with a spouse or a good friend.
- Read a biography, novel, or magazine (something other than what you read for work); take a nap or watch some television.

- Do something creative like painting, writing a poem, gardening, practicing a musical instrument, or knitting a sweater.
- Visit a zoo.
- Do the crossword puzzle in the newspaper or a Sudoku puzzle— or a jigsaw puzzle.
- Make a list of the "Top Ten Things I'm Grateful For."
- Plan a meal you've always wanted to try—and then cook it.
- Go out jogging or shoot a few hoops of basketball.
- Catch up with a friend or relative on the telephone.
- Take a neighbor, nephew, or niece out to the movies or invite someone over to watch a televised sports event.
- Spend time in prayer or spiritual reading.
- Listen to one of your favorite podcasts.

We enter into the authentic spirit of Sabbath rest when we choose a project or task that we enjoy *doing*; that makes it different from a project that we enjoy getting done. Without always being aware of the benefits, we find our lives get mended and time gets "collected" in the process of the doing. We begin to feel whole again; we catch our breath and anticipate the coming week. This spiritual practice was custom-made for humankind and is about a life-giving form of recreation as we celebrate Christ's re-creation at Easter.

Though the spiritual practice of Sabbath rest traditionally refers to an entire day, it can also be celebrated in short blocks of time during the week when we find ourselves running out of gas or spinning out of control. The stereotypical boss or inner voice might bark, "Don't just stand there—*do something*!" And yet the spiritual tradition of Sabbath rest responds, "Don't just do something— *stand there*." Take a break. Stop and relax. Taking such Sabbath time becomes another way of stoking the fire of godly enthusiasm as we respond to Jesus's invitation to turn off at a rest stop: "Come away to a deserted place all by yourselves and rest a while" (Mark 6:31). In those moments, we discover the rest and refreshment that only the Lord can give (see Matthew 11:28–30).

■ PRACTICE

Spend a large portion of a day, or even an entire day if your circumstances permit, doing nothing but relaxing and resting. Just lollygag and dawdle. Unless you like to cook, consider treating yourself to a meal out. If finances permit, invite a friend and go to a day spa. Don't journal about this. Don't reflect upon it. Just enjoy!

CHAPTER 35

PILGRIMAGE

■

I knelt in prayer in the small church of San Damiano, located outside the city walls of Assisi, Italy. This was where Francis of Assisi, early in the process of his spiritual transformation, prayed for guidance, direction, and insight. The earliest biographies state he heard a voice from the crucifix saying, "Francis, rebuild my church, which as you see is falling into ruin." That was the spark that set him ablaze and transformed him into a beacon of light for a smoldering medieval Church.

I had come from the suburbs of Chicago to this little Italian church on pilgrimage. Like Francis, I too was looking for guidance, direction, and insight, and I could think of no better place to seek them than in this little church that was so influential in Francis's life. I was completing my doctoral studies and was discerning my ministry: a professor in the classroom or a preacher on the road?

I spent the afternoon in that church. I prayed, reflected, read the story of Jesus calling his disciples in the fifth chapter of Luke's Gospel, and journaled. I didn't hear any heavenly voice as Francis had. But my pilgrimage to San Damiano did give me an insight that illumined my discernment process and has shaped me for the past thirty-five years: God speaks in the events of my life; it is important that I be attentive and reflect upon them—now, more than ever.

An Ancient Practice

Perhaps it is asking a lot for you to consider committing to pilgrimage as an important step on your journey of transformation. But I am nevertheless asking you to consider it—for centuries of reasons.

Going on pilgrimage is a spiritual practice that dates back to the ancient church. For the better part of two millennia, Christian pilgrims have traveled to the land of Jesus's life and death not only to encounter the sacred places of our faith but also to be challenged by Jesus's call to become his disciples. The spiritual practice of pilgrimage soon expanded to praying at the tombs of Peter and Paul in Rome, walking the *camino* (road) to the tomb of the apostle James in Santiago de Compostela in Spain, and visiting places made special by the lives of Francis of Assisi (Italy), Ignatius of Loyola (Spain), Juan Diego (Mexico), Bernadette Soubirous (France), Junipero Serra (United States), André Bessette (Canada), and hundreds of other saintly men and women.

Just because we travel to another place doesn't mean we are going on pilgrimage. Indeed, there are several significant differences between tourists and pilgrims. Tourists depart with passports, laptops, cell phones with cameras, and credit cards in hand. Prepared against any inconvenience and hoping to avoid any hassle, tourists travel accompanied by family and sometimes friends with the express purpose of seeing Arizona's Grand Canyon, London's Buckingham Palace, or Rome's Coliseum. Their trip is enhanced with leisurely visits to galleries, museums, cafés, and souvenir shops. In short, it's a vacation.

Pilgrims, on the other hand, though they might look like tourists on the surface, are really explorers. Their journey to a different place is really an interior journey to a deeper place. They leave the familiar exterior surroundings of their home to go to often unfamiliar surroundings within. This interior journey might prove to be like the physical journey with its own inconvenience, loss of control, and adaptation to new customs and languages. For some who just recently began to catch the fire of godly enthusiasm, the unfamiliar landscapes of their own souls might mirror the sometimes exotic scenes outside.

Pilgrims bring their Bibles and journals; they don't primarily travel to sightsee but to "soulsee"—to self-explore, to reflect, and to open themselves more deeply to the transforming process of the Spirit. That was the purpose of my pilgrimage to San Damiano. I could have easily gone soulseeing at home—I often do so!—but some locations are thin places (I briefly mentioned their significance in chapter 10) that have the power to open us to God's presence in unique and unforeseeable ways.

Pilgrims often travel with other pilgrims, with whom they gradually form a community that reflects the pilgrim church on earth. As such, they spend time praying both alone and communally. Rather than being encouraged to invest in souvenirs, pilgrims are challenged to divest themselves so that they can be molded in a truer way into the image of Christ. Their departure and journey to a sacred site, filled with self-reflection, prayer, and sometimes inconveniences and hassles, are *just as important* as their arrival.

The Practice of Pilgrimage

Unlike the motivation to visit an all-inclusive resort in Bali or an ancient monument like Stonehenge—relaxation, curiosity, adventure—the practice of pilgrimage begins with a spiritual desire, a call. I felt drawn to the little church of San Damiano because of its sacred significance in my Franciscan tradition and its potential for stoking the fire of godly enthusiasm in my life. Other pilgrims want to pray on the Mount of the Beatitudes; in the Garden of Gethsemane; on LaVerna, where Saint Francis received the stigmata; or at the grotto where the Blessed Mother appeared at Lourdes. We feel called to go to sacred sites to pray for others, to give thanks, to fulfill a promise, to ask for forgiveness, or to pray for a miracle.

Preparation. Pilgrimage begins with prayer and penance. To be led to a spiritual place within, we spend time in reflection, getting in touch with our spiritual desire to travel to a sacred place. If you are going to the Holy Land, you might want to read through one of the Gospels to refresh your memory about the significance of various places in Jesus's life. If you are visiting a shrine made popular by a saint's life, it's wise to read about the saintly virtue of the person ahead of time. In preparation for my pilgrimage to Assisi, I read the earliest account of the life of Saint Francis, written two years after his death.

A day or two before leaving, Catholic pilgrims might want to attend Mass and celebrate the Sacrament of Reconciliation in preparation for the upcoming spiritual journey.

The way of the pilgrim. We do not set out on our spiritual journey anticipating sumptuous food, comfortable transportation, and five-star hotels. We travel instead with the missionary spirit suggested by Jesus: detached, unencumbered, willing to accept any accommodation and whatever food is set before us (see Luke 9:1–5; 10:8). Pilgrimage also requires a lot of physical walking, which can be both challenging and exhausting. We presume

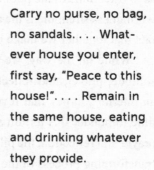

Carry no purse, no bag, no sandals. . . . Whatever house you enter, first say, "Peace to this house!". . . . Remain in the same house, eating and drinking whatever they provide.

Luke 10:4, 5, 7

that glitches and difficulties will occur; when they do, we notice our immediate reactions. The pilgrim's way challenges us to be patient, gentle with ourselves, and ever attentive and aware of the interior depths we are discovering while on the exterior journey to our pilgrim site. What happens *as* we travel *is* pilgrimage and forms an important part of this spiritual practice.

Along with patient, gentle self-awareness, we are called to foster three other attitudes. The first is to let go of any expectations. Those who deliberately seek out spiritual experiences and emotional highs will inevitably be disappointed; the God who journeyed with the Israelites in the desert and took on flesh in the forgotten town of Bethlehem has proven to be a God of surprise and disguise. While on the train from Rome to Assisi, I told myself not to expect the San Damiano crucifix to speak to me as it had to Francis; I knew that expectations turn a pilgrimage into an expedition and cause us to miss the grace that often catches us off guard in the present moment.

Another pilgrim attitude is the willingness to receive and offer acts of charity. As pilgrims, we are humble enough to receive hospitality from locals and allow them to attend to our needs. We are also generous enough to aid those in our group needing help as well as to offer alms to the poor and needy we encounter on the way. This willingness strengthens the awareness of our interdependence and the fact that together we make up the body of Christ.

While on the way, we make a concerted effort to find time for solitude, prayer, and reflection. Making a pilgrimage is essentially an interior journey that reveals the geography of the soul. We need time to ponder this terrain and discover its burning bushes. Without prayer and reflection, the pilgrimage loses its potential and power as a transforming process of the Spirit.

Arrival. If we have been faithful to self-awareness, having few expectations and having humility, generosity, and prayer while on pilgrimage, our arrival at the sacred site will be symbolic of a new interior place in which we find ourselves. And with the new interior place comes a new potential for transformation.

While at the sacred site, we pray with any Scripture passage associated with the setting. Through the practice of imaginative prayer discussed in chapter 17, we can place ourselves at the commemorated event. Afterward, to preserve the memory of the experience, we can journal about the emotions that arose, what we discovered about God and ourselves, and what spiritual challenge or gift this site offered to us.

Praying at the tomb of holy men and women, we ask the Holy Spirit to transform us into the image of Christ sent to lovingly respond to the unmet need or required duty of the present moment. We ask the saints to intercede and help us surrender, as they did, to the Spirit's promptings and process.

Returning Home. We keep the memory of the pilgrimage alive by listening closely to Gospel readings at Mass. A site is mentioned, and we can say, "I was there!" We can also honor again the particular saint of the day. It's helpful to occasionally reread pilgrimage journals. Such practices keep us mindful that the God who has a burning desire to be in a relationship with us has himself come down on pilgrimage in the sacrament of the present moment.

And when we find ourselves physically incapable or financially unable to make another pilgrimage to a specific destination, we can rediscover the purpose of pilgrimage right where we are by walking again the interior highway of the heart to Mt. Zion in prayer (see Psalm 84:5).

■ PRACTICE

Spend time reflecting upon the sacred sites and places of pilgrimage that you feel drawn to. If one of them is local, consider an afternoon pilgrimage to it. If they are associated with Jesus or the early disciples in the Middle East, spend time with the appropriate Scripture passage; if with a saint, read about the person. If finances permit, commit to getting information and making a pilgrimage. If finances do not permit, visit a local bookstore or a virtual bookstore like Amazon and buy a pictorial guide to the place. Engage the location with the imaginative prayer technique mentioned in chapter 17 or use the method of visio divina mentioned in chapter 16 with a work of art.

CHAPTER 36

HOSPITALITY

∎

I have more than 1.5 million frequent flyer points on United Airlines. I've crisscrossed the country hundreds of times to preach parish missions and retreats to clergy, religious, and laity. As an itinerant preacher who spends more nights in guest rooms than in my friary bedroom, I have been dependent upon the hospitality of others and have discovered that some people glow with a welcoming spirit in ways beyond all telling.

As a path to spiritual transformation, hospitality is more than putting chocolate on the pillow, fresh towels in the bathroom, or having freshly brewed coffee available in the morning. It is a spiritual practice that demands self-forgetfulness and attention to the guest's needs that few people have mastered. What are some of the qualities of a host that can lead to their spiritual transformation?

Acceptance

There's no template for hospitality because each guest arrives with his or her own baggage, both physical and emotional. But in its most basic expression, an authentic welcome begins with an open, accepting heart. My frequent flights to Singapore have been a grueling 19-hour flight via Houston and Tokyo. Upon my arrival typically between midnight and 1 a.m., my breath smells awful and my face is scratchy with whiskers. But neither stops my dear friends Benny and Sandra from welcoming me with open arms and a warm, prolonged bear hug. These friends overlook what I consider the elephant in the room and simply delight in my presence. I chuckle and relish the bottle of Australian red wine that always waits opened and breathing on the dining room table. I've learned I won't be going to bed until we have gotten caught up on recent events since my last visit and emails.

Accommodations

Occasionally I am asked what the most challenging aspect of my life as an itinerant preacher is. I always note the surprise on people's faces when I reply, "Living in rectory guestrooms." I know it sounds superficial and trite—but it's true. When you spend as much time in guestrooms as I do, you come to lower your expectations. So many rectory guestrooms have become the cemetery for VCR players from the 1980s and old computer monitors. Two or three statues of the Virgin Mary and an occasional St. Joseph standing guard over the chest of drawers are typically adorned with plastic flowers, remnants of a card party hosted by the Ladies Guild. There's at least one version of the Peace Prayer of St. Francis written in calligraphy and framed, or Praying Hands cross-stitched on a pillow. And then there is the closet, filled with old clothes and vestments and sometimes sweaters, still in their boxes, given with appreciation at Christmas and received with less enthusiasm. The bed is sometimes salvaged from a closed convent and sometimes donated by a parishioner moving out of the parish. The small desk that matches the chest of drawers is typically more for looks than for use. There's a one-out-of-four chance I'll have a recliner to sit in; if not, a straight-backed chair will be negotiated into a corner and will need to be moved if I want to use it.

None of that was the case at Fr. Damian's parish in Florida. "Please, make yourself at home," he said as he opened the guestroom door, "and if you need anything whatsoever, don't hesitate to ask me." I immediately noticed some details that set his hospitality apart from others'. First, there was the personal, handwritten note of welcome that included the wifi password. Two different kinds of

Be hospitable to
one another without
complaining. Like
good stewards of the
manifold grace of God,
serve one another with
whatever gift each of
you has received.

1 Peter 4:9–10

unopened soap bars with two bottles of traveler's size shampoo had been artfully placed alongside the towels on the bed. There was also a basket containing toothpaste, toothbrushes, Q-tip swabs, dental floss, and combs. I noticed the room was exceptionally clean and simply appointed, a sign that it was meant to be lived in and not simply admired. "If I've missed anything or if you have any other needs, I hope you will tell me," Fr. Damian said as he left me to unpack and settle in. "I'll be back in thirty minutes to give you the grand tour of the church and rectory." I felt pampered and welcomed by a host who must have known the challenges of being a guest.

Table of Plenty

It's always music to my ears when I hear Mary Ann announce, "Come to the table!" A guest never *eats* at her table; one can only *dine*. This maestro orchestrates a cantata of care and affection as she delicately sets her table: the placement of the dishes and utensils sings sotto voce of her cordial and gracious spirit. The food and its careful presentation provide the chorus of love.

To dine at Mary Ann's table is to be reminded that spiritual transformation can occur as one lovingly stirs the homemade pasta sauce and labors not to burn the loaf of bread in the oven. For many people like Mary Ann, the kitchen is a sanctuary where Martha's hands and Mary's heart meet among the pots and pans.

Availability

As a guest in rectories in unfamiliar cities, I often feel imprisoned by the guest room and lack of transportation. As I wait for the evening's preaching engagement, I sometimes struggle with boredom and loneliness. Even though I have learned how to keep myself occupied while on the road with prayer, reading, and writing, somedays the sun seems a bit hesitant and bullheaded to move. I sit in the guestroom watching the clock and waiting for sunset.

Occasionally I'll be with a priest, nun, or minister who knows the challenges I face as an itinerant preacher and will go out of their way to entertain me and keep me occupied. Sr. Rose, a native of Sydney, Australia, immediately comes to mind. As superior of her congregation's retirement center, housing some 53 elderly and infirm sisters, she daily faces a full schedule as she arranges transportation for medical appointments, visits the bedridden, meets with the head of maintenance, and supervises various other tasks. "Father," she said as she whisked by with the pace of a nurse in Intensive Care, "as you Yanks say, I'm not sure if I'm coming or going—but wish me a safe trip, nevertheless!" Before I could open my mouth, she disappeared at the turn of the corridor.

A dedicated worker bee, Sr. Rose still made time to hover over me. Every morning, she knocked on my door and asked the same question, "Do you have any needs today?" Two times during the week, she came to my room and announced, "Get your jacket. It's chilly outside. We're going for a ride." Every evening around 7 p.m., she showed up with ice cream. "I have chocolate, vanilla, and strawberry. Do you want just one or a taste of all three?" It's an understatement to say, but despite her busy schedule, Sr. Rose was hospitality incarnated.

Guest Rules

As a guest, I am aware I can be an intrusion in the life of a host. I've learned that my life as a guest can also be a spiritual practice if I follow some basic guest etiquette. Some rules that I try to keep in mind and follow include these:

- *Don't be demanding when it comes to food.* Jesus knows the desire for his favorite food after a long day of walking and no doubt working up an appetite. Yet, when he sends his disciples out on mission, he instructs them, "Whenever you enter a town and its people welcome you, eat what is set before you . . ." (Luke 10:8) Paul gives similar advice to the Corinthians: "If an unbeliever invites you to a meal and you are disposed to go, eat whatever is set before you without raising any question on the ground of conscience" (1 Corinthians 10:27).

  I remember being invited to an interdenominational church in South Carolina for a day of talks during Lent. I arrived on Friday, and that evening, the minister's wife had prepared some delicious stuffed pork chops. Though Catholics are to abstain from meat on Fridays of Lent, I still remember just how tasty those pork chops were.

- *Inquire about house policies and procedures.* Should I lock the door when I leave for my daily walk? Should I leave dirty dishes in the sink or rinse them and put them in the dishwasher? Is it okay for me to watch television in the living room? May I use the washing machine to wash my dirty clothes before I leave? As basic as these questions are, they show a real interest in not being a nuisance or an unwelcome guest. Sensitivity to surroundings is a practical way of respecting the host and forgetting myself.

- *Respect the host's duties and obligations.* It's important that the host doesn't feel burdened or overwhelmed by my presence. Just like me, the host needs some personal space to rest and relax.

- *Lend a helping hand.* Offer to set the table, remove the dishes after a meal, help with the dishwashing, or load the dishwasher. As a guest, I am never exempt from responding to the unmet need or required duty of the present moment or doing acts of charity.

- *Dress appropriately.* It can be a real temptation to dress down while in the host's space. Though I prefer to go barefoot while inside my bedroom, I never, ever go barefoot in public areas.

- *Don't leave a mess behind.* Cleaning up after myself is a practical way to show respect to the host. This includes making the bed each morning and stripping the bed before I leave. I never presume maid service.

- *Treat the host to his or her favorite meal or bottle of wine.* I am never exempt from showing gratitude.

- *Respect the morning and evening rituals of the host.* It's important to know if the host is an early bird or night owl. That will affect my time in front of the television and the use of my laptop.

- *Express gratitude for the hospitality received.* Writing a thank you note, sending an email, or following up with a phone call after departure are all ways of expressing appreciation and thanks. And it's a nice touch to be specific. For example, "I really appreciated you driving me to the airport at such an early hour" or "Thanks so much for treating me to that terrific Chinese restaurant."

In chapter 53 of his Rule, Saint Benedict of Nursia reminds us that hospitality is a spiritual practice. He writes that every guest should be welcomed as Christ and quotes Matthew 25:35, "For I was a stranger and you welcomed me." The challenge for every guest is to be Christlike and worthy of such a welcome.

■ PRACTICE

Look at your guest room. How welcoming and comfortable is it? What changes could be made to it to enhance a guest's visit? Consider making those changes.

If you are a cook, consider making your favorite meal and inviting someone to your table. Remember that the very act of meal preparation is a spiritual practice if you attend to it with sensitivity, care, concern, and love for your guest.

CHAPTER 37

LIVING IN THE PRESENT MOMENT

∎

A Capuchin Franciscan friar relished telling me a funny story about Saint Padre Pio of Pietrelcina and his mystical gift of being in two places at once called "bilocation." One day, the guardian (religious superior) of the Franciscan community entered the refectory while Padre Pio was enjoying a cup of coffee. "Padre Pio," the guardian excitedly exclaimed, "you'll never believe this. I just heard on the radio that a plane flew from Rome to New York in just under twelve hours!" Unimpressed, Padre Pio looked up at the guardian and wryly replied, "Father, when I fly to New York, it takes me a split second!"

In the Past, In the Future

I sometimes wonder if all of us have Padre Pio's gift of bilocation. Most of us are in one physical location, but mentally we are somewhere else. Some of us are stuck in the past, still berating ourselves for some mistake or sin we committed. That's what guilt is all about. Others are stumbling into the future. That's what worry and anxiety are all about. It sounds strange to say it but most of us are not mentally where we are physically.

Newborn babies, on the other hand, don't know guilt, worry, or anxiety. All they know is the present moment. A newborn baby sees something funny and he laughs. She is hungry and she cries. But as newborns grow up, they *learn* guilt when a parent tells them, "You're in big trouble!" They *learn* worry and anxiety as they prepare for quizzes and tests or hear their parents fuss over finances. Guilt, worry, and anxiety are not natural. They are learned behaviors.

Truly I tell you,
unless you change
and become like
children, you will
never enter the
kingdom of heaven.

Matthew 18:3

So much of Jesus's ministry was focused on getting people to unlearn guilt, worry, and anxiety. Jesus forgave sins and freed people from their past (Matthew 9:6, Luke 7:47; 23:34) so they could be where they physically were. He urged his followers to live in the present moment and not worry about tomorrow (Matthew 6:34). He challenged each listener to return to being a child and rediscover the present moment.

The Sacrament of the Present Moment

The mid-nineteenth century gave birth to one of the great classics of Christian spirituality, *Abandonment to Divine Providence*. Contemporary scholars are uncertain who the author was though tradition has ascribed it to the eighteenth-century Jesuit Jean-Pierre de Caussade. Sometimes compared to the mystical works of John of the Cross and Teresa of Avila, *Abandonment to Divine Providence* offers a practical mysticism of the present moment.

The text calls the present moment a "sacrament."[36] The present moment is a thin place, the portal through which God and angels enter our lives. Think of the Lord's visit to Abraham and receiving hospitality at the patriarch's tent in Mamre (Genesis 18:1–33). Remember Gabriel's visit and invitation to Mary (Luke 1:26–38)? Devout Simeon was riveted to the present moment and recognized divine "light for revelation . . . for glory" when Joseph and Mary presented Jesus in the Temple (Luke 2:25–35). The years of prayer made the prophetess Anna so prayerful that she too recognized the child who would bring redemption (Luke 2:36–38). Those who consciously live with attention to the present moment often recognize and encounter a divine visitation.

There is another reason why the present moment is sacramental. In the words of the text, "Every moment we live through is like an ambassador who declares the will of God."[37] To be attentive to the present moment is to discover God's plan for me right here, right now. And that divine will and plan are made manifest in the unmet need or required duty of the present moment: the outstretched hand of a poor person, the cry of an infant, the twinge of conscience to forgive a neighbor. By responding to this unmet need or required duty before me, I fan God's spark into flame. In the words of *Abandonment to Divine Providence*, "What was the best thing for us to do in the moment that has passed is no longer so, for the will of God is now manifesting itself in those circumstances which are the duty of the present moment. It is the fulfilling of this duty, no matter in what guise it presents itself, which does most to make one holy."[38]

Listening to the Ambassador

While I was being interviewed about living in the present moment on a national Catholic talk radio show, a caller from Los Angeles raised an objection that I often hear. "Father Albert," she said, "I'm a single parent with two children. I can't afford to dillydally in the present moment. I must be concerned about putting food on the table next week, paying my children's tuition next month, and continuing to support myself. It would be irresponsible and maybe even reckless to practice what you are suggesting."

The host of the show allowed me to respond to the caller's objection. "I think you might have misunderstood what I am saying," I replied and continued, "I agree with you that it *would* be irresponsible and reckless not to be concerned about the future. But that's not what I am saying. I'm suggesting that you allow the present moment—this ambassador of God's will—to tell you what you should be doing right now. If the present moment is calling you to look over last month's charges and pay your credit card bill or examine your conscience for the sacrament of reconciliation, then you live in the past and do what you need to do. If the present moment is calling you to live in the future, plan your meal menu in preparation for grocery shopping, then you live in the future and do just that. It's not about choosing between the past, the present, or the future. Rather, it's about allowing the ambassador of the present moment to declare to you what is God's will—and what needs to be done."

A Four-Step Method

Many contemporary writers and spiritual teachers have been telling us about the importance of living in the present moment. But no one has told us *how* to do it. A few years ago, I developed a simple four-step method that can be remembered with the acronym RARA.

Begin with *recollection*. "Re-collect" yourself from all the many places where you might currently be bilocating—whether in the past or the future. This can be facilitated by closing your eyes for a few seconds, taking a few deep breaths, then opening your eyes as you ask yourself, "Where am I?" Simply respond to your question with "Right here, right now."

Continue with *attention*. Be attentive to your five senses and what they are registering right now. Notice the cardinal in the tree. Feel the softness of the newborn's skin. Listen to the horses galloping. Taste the hamburger. Put your nose to the freshly cut rose. Don't rush this step because your five senses are the key that opens the tabernacle to the sacrament of the present moment.

The third step is *reflection*. What is God's will for you as you consider and mull over the present moment? What is this moment's unmet need or required duty? To do an act of charity? To simply enjoy the moment? To change your child's diaper? To put clothes in the dryer? To say a prayer of gratitude or thanksgiving?

Conclude with *action*. Having returned to the here-and-now, attended to what your senses are telling you about it, and taken into consideration what this ambassador is asking of you, you now respond.

This four-step method is not intended to be a twenty-minute technique. I find myself doing it for two minutes at most, five or six times a day—whenever I catch myself bilocating, or waiting for a green light, or taking a walk, or being tempted to check my email again. The more you are willing to practice the method consistently, the more living in the present moment will become a habit. Gradually that habit will become second nature. And then you'll surprise yourself by suddenly being right where you are and responding to God's will in the unmet need or required duty of the present moment!

A New Interpretation of a Well-Known Parable

We all are familiar with the parable of the judgment of the nations (Matthew 25:31–46). The Son of Man returns and separates people one from another as a shepherd separates the sheep from the goats. When the Son of Man sends the goats to the eternal fire prepared for the devil and his minions because they did not respond to his hunger, thirst, need for hospitality, nakedness, sickness, or imprisonment, they protest with the question, "Lord, when was it that we saw you hungry, or thirsty, or a stranger or naked or sick or in prison, and did not take care of you?" (v. 44). We can all quote from memory the famous line spoken to them, "Truly I tell you, just as you did not do it to one of the least of these, you did not do it to me" (v. 45). The parable is often interpreted as highlighting the importance of seeing Christ in the poor and needy.

However, there is another valid interpretation if we focus on the sheep. The Son of Man invites the sheep to inherit the kingdom for this reason: "[F]or I was hungry and you gave me food, I was thirsty and you gave me something to drink, I was a stranger and you welcomed me, I was naked and you gave me clothing, I was sick and you took care of me, I was in prison and you visited me" (v. 35–36). The sheep must have been stunned, for they ask the question that the goats will subsequently ask, "Lord, when was it that we saw you hungry and gave you food, or thirsty and gave you something to drink? And when was it that we saw you a stranger and welcomed you, or naked and gave you clothing? And when was it that we saw you sick or in prison and visited you?" (v. 37–39) The Son of Man surprises them with the great reveal, "Truly I tell you, just as you did it to one of the least of these who are members of my family, you did it to me" (v. 40). Notice the sheep did not "see" the Son of Man in the hungry, thirsty, stranger, naked, sick, or imprisoned. Rather, they were living in the present moment and simply responding to the unmet need or required duty before them. And without even knowing it, by responding to the need or duty, the sheep, like Abraham, Mary, Simeon, and Anna, discover the present moment suddenly transformed into a thin place, an encounter with the divine.

A Prayer

I wrote a prayer to conclude my radio interview about living in the present moment. When you find yourself distracted or discouraged by your bilocation tendencies, consider praying:

O Loving Father,
You speak me into existence at this very moment
And want me to enjoy
The sights, sounds, smells, tastes, and feelings
Of this lush garden called the here-and-now.
And yet, I am exiled from the present moment
Because I choose to live in the past,

Berating myself for sins committed
Or sunk in regret for roads not taken.
Sometimes I live in the future
And insult you with my worries, concerns, and anxieties.
Help me to find my way home to the sacrament of the present
    moment.

Jesus, Son of the Father,
You free me from my past
By your ministry of forgiveness and reconciliation
And you pull me from my fears and worries about the future
By challenging me to trust in your Father's protection and
    providence.
Help me to boldly stand renewed and refreshed
Right here.

Spirit of love,
Awaken and enlighten me to the divine will manifested
In the outstretched hand, the infant's cry, and the stranger's plea,
Knowing that when I respond to the least of these standing before
    me
I am responding to you.
Give me the grace to know
That this moment—every moment!—
Is a sacred moment
And your grace can transform me
If only I but live here and now
And lovingly respond to whatever is before me.
Amen.

The present moment is the divine ambassador that declares God's will for us. Living in it gives birth to our sense of mission as the Spirit transforms us into the image of Christ sent to lovingly respond to this moment's unmet need or required duty. Our response lifts the veil on the here-and-now and surprises us with the revelation of the divine.

■ PRACTICE

Commit to living in the present moment tomorrow. Perhaps write on a few Post-it Notes, "Recollect, attend, reflect, act." Stick one note on your bathroom mirror, another on the refrigerator, still another on your computer monitor or smart device, and one on your television set. Whenever you notice the note, practice the four-step method for two minutes. In the evening, assess its help and viability for you.

CHAPTER 38

SOUL TRAINING

∎

Fire and the heat that radiates from it cleanse and sterilize imperfections and impurities from an object as it is being transformed. The same is true for us as we become more and more Christlike by the power of the Holy Spirit. That's why there's another commitment you need to consider, and it might just be one of the most challenging of all.

Stephen, a spiritual directee of mine, once asked, "What's the purpose of doing penance and acts of asceticism? Sometimes I do them to express sorrow for my sins; but then there are other times when I think of them as a kind of spiritual workout or soul training. Which is correct?"

Stephen's question gave me cause to pause and reconsider the motivation and intention behind all spiritual practices.

The Purpose of Practice

There is a wide range of spiritual practices: different methods of prayer, the examination of conscience, journaling, and pilgrimage, to name just a few of the ones we've explored in these pages. These practices do not make God present, for God pervades our very existence like the air we breathe: "In [God] we live and move and have our being" (Acts 17:28). Instead, they help to deepen our awareness of God and foster sensitivity to the "fullness of him who fills all in all" (Ephesians 1:23): the divine presence within us as well as the divine presence we encounter in the sacraments, in Scripture, in creation, in the events of our lives, and in our neighbor. In effect, they stoke the fire of godly enthusiasm and help to keep it burning in our lives.

CATCHING FIRE, BECOMING FLAME

Acts of penance and asceticism have their own traditional place within the range of spiritual practices. Acts of penance are often done in response to the awareness of our sinfulness before the presence of God. Acts of asceticism are also forms of "soul training," to use Stephen's expression; that is, we practice them to strengthen ourselves against the false self and the ego-obsessions with self-concern, self-image, self-gratification, and self-preservation. The three great practices of penance and asceticism taught by Jesus are prayer, fasting, and almsgiving.

In the Gospel of Matthew, Jesus places these three practices at the very center of the Sermon on the Mount. We are to give alms in secret so that we do not receive the praise of others (see 6:2–4). Prayer should be direct, succinct, and done behind closed doors (see 6:5–8). Fasting, like almsgiving and prayer, should not call attention to itself or be noticed by others (see 6:16–18). Though Jesus tells us *how* they should be practiced—in secret, not calling attention to themselves— he remains silent on *why* they should be practiced.

But Jesus's Jewish tradition would have provided the reasons for prayer, fasting, and almsgiving. The Hebrew Scriptures are filled with references to the prayers of thanksgiving, confession, petition, and intercession (see, e.g., 2 Kings 6:17; Psalm 95:2; Daniel 9:3–21; Sirach 51:13); the multitude of references all suggest prayer as our method of communicating with God. Fasting is a way to express contrition and a sincere intent to change one's ways (see, for example, 1 Samuel 7:6; Jonah 3:5); Isaiah broadened its understanding to express a desire to turn away from injustice against, oppression of, and insensitivity toward the poor and needy (see, for example, Isaiah 58:6–7). Almsgiving makes us aware of the interdependence between us and the poor, the foreigners, the widows, and orphans (see Exodus 23:11; Deuteronomy 14:29).

Restoring Harmony

I value and respect the time-honored Jewish rationale for the three traditional practices of penance and asceticism—communication with God, conversion, and awareness of our interdependence. But I think there's another reason we should intentionally commit to these practices.

The Garden of Eden is the biblical symbol for the way God created this world and intended it to be. All of creation was intricately connected and interdependent. Naked Adam and Eve felt no shame before each other and naturally experienced the presence of God in the "evening breeze" (Genesis 3:8). In this paradise, there was harmony and balance among God, self, and others.

But at some point, the false self with its obsessive self-centered desires made its appearance. "The woman saw that the tree was . . . to be desired to make one wise" (Genesis 3:6). And along with the first man's and woman's giving in to that desire, the natural awareness of God's presence was lost; it would now have to be practiced. Human beings began to experience shame, and competition arose in relationships. The original harmony was disrupted, and the balance was destroyed.

Though we do not have the ability to definitively heal the consequences of original sin, we are able to catch glimpses of the divine, original intention for harmony and balance among God, ourselves, and others. This is exactly what acts of penance and asceticism provide for us.

Not simply a way to communicate with God, prayer also makes us prayerful. It helps us to grow in sensitivity to and awareness of the divine presence that pervades all of life. And so it helps us to experience again what was once a natural part of the human condition, when God could be heard walking in the evening breeze.

Fasting keeps us in touch with ourselves and the physical way we get trapped in a shameful cycle of obsession with self-concern, self-image, self-gratification, and self-preservation. Though traditionally practiced with regard to food and drink, fasting can also be applied to internet sites, television shows, shopping, exercising, emails, and other forms of distraction and entertainment. Regular fasting helps to keep the false self in check.

Thus it is written, "The first man, Adam, became a living being"; the last Adam became a life-giving spirit. But it is not the spiritual that is first, but the physical, and then the spiritual. The first man was from the earth, a man of dust; the second man is from heaven. As was the man of dust, so are those who are of the dust; and as is the man of heaven, so are those who are of heaven. Just as we have borne the image of the man of dust, we will also bear the image of the man of heaven.

1 Corinthians 15:45–49

Almsgiving promotes the interdependence with others that God wove within the very fabric of human life. Sharing our financial treasures with others builds a bridge between us and those who have fewer resources and opportunities than we do. Sharing our time and our talents gives us the opportunity to celebrate our innate gifts and to build community. In a real way, this practice helps us to overcome the competitive stance many of us have toward others.

As we submit to the Spirit's transformative process and become more Christlike, we also become a new creation (see 2 Corinthians 5:17). Part of our newness, discovered through the traditional practices of prayer, fasting, and almsgiving, is experiencing the fullness of life that Christ, "the last Adam," now enjoys and that God intended for us from the very first day of creation.

▪ PRACTICE

Consider your upcoming week and commit to a day of soul training. Before choosing between prayer, fasting, or almsgiving, ask yourself: Do I need to strengthen my awareness of God's presence through prayer, challenge my obsession with the concerns of the false self through fasting, or reinforce my connection with others through almsgiving? Choose just one of the three practices for this day. At the end of the day, reflect upon your experience, perhaps journal about it, and then commit to another session of soul training next week.

A PRAYER AT THE HEARTH
OF THE HEART

■

Catching fire and becoming flame require more than the spark of the Spirit and our well-chosen kindling. They also demand an ongoing perseverance and long-term patience forged from the awareness that God fervently desires to see us blaze with godly enthusiasm. That enthusiasm flares up as we willingly surrender to the communal process of being transformed by the Spirit of God sent to lovingly respond to the unmet need or required duty of the present moment. We commit to and continue this spiritual transformation by praying these words every day:

O Loving God,
The fiery ardor of your enthusiasm to be in a relationship
    with me crackles in every event, person, insight, and
    longing you send along my way.
They are sparks thrown upon the kindling in my hearth.
    Ignite my heart with your living flame of love.

O Selfless Jesus,
your soul raged with the desire to set this world ablaze with
    the love, mercy, and compassion of your Abba.
Stoke my flame with the wisdom of the gospel
so that I might burn with the same fervor that fueled your
    life.

O Empowering Spirit,
you are the flint and fuel of God's love that enlightens my
        vision to see those who are in need
and impassions my heart to respond to the unmet need or
        required duty of the present moment.
Transform me so I might die for love of Christ's love,
he who was on fire to die for love of my love.

Amen.

A PERENNIAL METAPHOR

■

Even a cursory look through the Bible reveals the close association between God and fire. In the covenant with Abram, God appears as a "smoking fire pot and a flaming torch" (Genesis 15:17). "[I]n a flame of fire out of a bush" (Exodus 3:2), God reveals to Moses divine compassion for the Israelites in Egypt and the divine name. During the Exodus, a pillar of fire by night is the outward sign of God's guiding presence (see Exodus 13:21; Numbers 14:14). God descends upon Mount Sinai "in fire" (Exodus 19:18). The prophets Ezekiel (1:27) and Daniel (7:9) describe the fire surrounding God's throne while the Book of Revelation places "a sea of glass mixed with fire" (Revelation 15:2) before it. Revelation also mentions "seven flaming torches, which are the seven spirits of God" (Revelation 4:5) before this throne. The psalmist sings, "The voice of the Lord flashes forth flames of fire" (Psalm 29:7). Daniel writes that "a stream of fire issued and flowed out from [God's] presence" (Daniel 7:10) and his "man clothed in linen" whom the early church referenced as the glorified Jesus has eyes "like flaming torches" (Daniel 10:6). Revelation's Son of Man has eyes "like a flame of fire" (Revelation 1:14, 2:18). The Letter to the Hebrews states that God's servants are "flames of fire" (1:7) and explicitly proclaims, "[F]or indeed our God is a consuming fire" (12:29). Jesus spoke of his mission as bringing "fire to the earth" (Luke 12:49). In the Acts of the Apostles, the Holy Spirit descends upon the gathered community like tongues "as of fire" (Acts 2:3).

Since the first edition of *Catching Fire, Becoming Flame: A Guide for Spiritual Transformation* in 2013, I have become especially sensitive to these biblical references. They convince me that "catching fire" is an apt metaphor for the process of spiritual transformation for which we all yearn. We prepare kindling with our attitudes of openness, acceptance, and surrender that we place under the wood of the cross given to us. In God's blazing desire to have a deeper relationship with us, God throws a spark into our lives. And then God waits to see if we fan that divine spark into flame with spiritual practices. When we do, that flame rises in our hearts as we watch our ego-obsessions gradually go up in smoke. The divine consuming fire begins to blaze, rage, and roar in our hearts while igniting within us love for the things of heaven, the wonders of creation, and the people of earth. Anointed with tongues "as of fire," we become "flames of fire" as the Letter to the Hebrews mentions, and with Jesus, we are called to bring God's fiery enthusiasm to earth. We express this mission in our loving response to the unmet need or required duty of the present moment.

The fourteenth-century Dominican mystic Meister Eckhart succinctly captured this process of spiritual transformation when he preached, "Fire transforms all things it touches into its own nature. The wood does not change the fire but the fire changes the wood into itself. In the same way we are transformed into God."[39] And with that transformation, the smoldering ashes of our self-centered lives are extinguished as we crackle with selfless love.

ACKNOWLEDGMENTS

I am deeply grateful to the people who attend not only my workshops on prayer and the spiritual life but also my parish missions and retreats. Ten years ago, their enthusiasm for these ideas motivated me to write this book and develop its two DVDs, now streaming videos.

I also am grateful for the close collaboration that has developed with Paraclete Press and the Community of Jesus because of this book and its DVDs. I have since published two other books with Paraclete Press and filmed three other streaming videos. I was filled with excitement when Paraclete Press allowed me to revise and expand my thoughts on the spiritual life with this tenth anniversary edition of *Catching Fire, Becoming Flame: A Guide for Spiritual Transformation*. Thanks to all who made this happen.

I would be remiss if I did not specifically mention Bob Edmonson of the Community of Jesus. I have fond memories of his hospitality and graciousness the first time I visited the Community of Jesus on Cape Cod to film the first two DVDs for this book. Bob's meticulous skill for formatting pages, editing, and proofreading are second to none. As an author, I have come to implicitly trust his judgment—and that has made my ministry as a writer so much easier. Thank you, Bob!

■

Ordained a Franciscan priest in 1983, Albert Haase, OFM, is a popular preacher and teacher. A former missionary to mainland China for over eleven years, he is the award-winning author of thirteen books on popular spirituality and the presenter on five bestselling DVDs. He currently resides in San Antonio TX. Visit his website at www.AlbertOFM.org

NOTES

1   Pope Francis, *Rejoice and Be Glad: On the Call to Holiness in Today's World,* paragraph 11.

2   Saint John of the Cross, *The Dark Night,* Book 2, chapter 10, paragraph 1.

3   M. Robert Mulholland's classic definition of spiritual formation is "the process of being conformed to the image of Christ for the sake of others." See M. Robert Mulholland, Jr., *Invitation to a Journey: A Road Map for Spiritual Formation* (Downers Grove, IL: InterVarsity Press, 1993), 15.

4   Augustine of Hippo, *Confessions,* Book 1, paragraph 1.

5   Rev. Francois Jamart, OCD, *Complete Spiritual Doctrine of St. Therese of Lisieux* (New York: Alba House, 1961), 16.

6   Augustine, *Sermo* 117.3.5.

7   Teresa of Avila, *Life*, chapter 8:5. The paraphrase is my own.

8   James Finley, *Merton's Palace of Nowhere* (Notre Dame, IN: Ave Maria Press, 1978), 114.

9   *Collected Works of G. K. Chesterton, Volume X: Collected Poetry: Part 1,* edited by Aidan Mackey (San Francisco: Ignatius Press, 1994), 43.

10   Donna Wilkinson, *The Only 127 Things You Need: A Guide to Life's Essentials* (New York: Tarcher, 2008), 347.

11   Meister Eckhart, *Sermon XXVII.*

12   Augustine, *Enarrationes in psalmos* 105.

13   Angela of Foligno, *Memorial* 55.

14   Meister Eckhart, "Talks of Instruction" 22.

15   Dennis Hamm, SJ, "Rummaging for God: Praying Backwards through Your Day," *America Magazine,* May 14, 1994.

16   Brother Lawrence of the Resurrection, *The Practice of the Presence of God. Spiritual Maxims,* chapter 6, paragraph 31.

17   John of the Cross, "The Ascent of Mount Carmel," stanza 5.

18   Benedict XVI, "Address of His Holiness, Benedict XVI, to the Participants in the International Congress Organized to Commemorate the 40th Anniversary of the Dogmatic Constitution on Divine Revelation, '*Dei Verbum*'," given at Castel Gondolfo, Friday, 16 September, 2005.

19   Saint Clare of Assisi, "Second Letter to Blessed Agnes of Prague," 20.

20   Douglas J. Leonhardt, SJ, "Gospel Contemplation," in *Finding God in All Things: A Marquette Prayer Book* (Milwaukee, WI: Marquette University Press, 2009).

21   Thomas of Celano, *Second Life*, #165.

22   Bernard of Clairvaux, *Epistles*, #106.

23   Meister Eckhart, Sermon 67.

24   Teresa of Avila, *Way of Perfection*, Chapters 21, 27; Chapter 29, paragraph 6; Chapter 31, paragraphs 3, 13.

25   Tertullian, *Prayer*, chapter 1, #6.

26   Bro. Don Bisson, "St. John of the Cross: Befriending the Dark Journey," (YesNowProductions: Audio MP3 Download), #31.

27   Saint John of the Cross, *The Dark Night*, Book 2, Chapter 2, paragraph 1.

28   Brian Kolodiejchuk, MC, ed., Mother Teresa, *Come Be My Light: The Private Writings of the "Saint of Calcutta"* (New York: Doubleday, 2007), 210.

29   The full interview can be found at Inés San Martín, "Family chooses forgiveness after drunk driver kills three of their children," at https://cruxnow.com/wmof/2022/06/family-chooses-forgiveness-after-drunk-driver-kills-three-of-their-children, June 25, 2022.

30   This prayer was reformatted and rewritten by Albert Haase, OFM. The original by an unknown author can be found at http://www.arlingtondiocese.org/Family-Life/Prayer-for-Inner-Healing.pdf.

31   Cathy Wright, LSJ, *Charles de Foucauld: Journey of the Spirit* (Boston: Pauline Books & Media, 2005), 78.

32   Henri Nouwen, *The Way of the Heart: The Spirituality of the Desert Fathers and Mothers* (New York: HarperOne, 1981), 27.

33   Paraphrase of Francis of Assisi, Admonition 19:2.

34   Nouwen, *The Way of the Heart*, 25.

35   Abraham Joshua Heschel, *The Sabbath: Its Meaning for Modern Man* (New York: Noonday Press, 1975), 18.

36   *Abandonment to Divine Providence*, Book 1, Chapter 1, Section 2.

37   *Abandonment to Divine Providence*, Book 1, Chapter 2, Section 10.

38   *Abandonment to Divine Providence*, Book 1, Chapter 1, Section 5.

39   Meister Eckhart, *Wandering Joy: Meister Eckhart's Mystical Philosophy*, Translation and Commentary by Reiner Schürmann (Great Barrington, MA: Lindisfarne Books, 2001), xiii.

ABOUT PARACLETE PRESS

PARACLETE PRESS is the publishing arm of the Cape Cod Benedictine community, the Community of Jesus. Presenting a full expression of Christian belief and practice, we reflect the ecumenical charism of the Community and its dedication to sacred music, the fine arts, and the written word.

SCAN
TO
READ
MORE

www.paracletepress.com